MINORITIES
in
TEXTBOOKS

A Study
of Their Treatment
in
Social Studies
Texts

by
MICHAEL B. KANE
Preface by Oscar Cohen

*Published in cooperation with the Anti-Defamation League of
B'nai B'rith by Quadrangle Books
Chicago*

To those who are forced to study from materials that ignore or misrepresent their heritage, in the hope that they will build a society whose schools value rather than suppress the differences among their children.

MINORITIES IN TEXTBOOKS.
Copyright © 1970 by the Anti-Defamation League of B'nai B'rith.
All rights reserved, including the right to reproduce this book or portions thereof in any form. For information, address: Quadrangle Books, Inc., 12 East Delaware Place, Chicago 60611. Manufactured in the United States of America. Published simultaneously in Canada by Burns and MacEachern Ltd., Toronto.

Library of Congress Catalog Card Number: 73-135871
SBN 8129-6138-2

PREFACE

It is not unreasonable to expect that, over twenty-one years, the readily admitted shortcomings of social studies textbooks in their treatment of racial, religious, and ethnic groups would have been corrected. But they have not. There have been some attempts to revise textbooks in order to overcome the objections of educators and others concerned with democratic practices, but these efforts have resulted only in minor improvements. Textbook publishers, who bear the major responsibility for this failure, must be prepared to accept the criticism arising from the revelations of this and other studies.

Of the numerous areas with which a study of textbooks could begin, one of the most obvious is the treatment of minorities in social studies texts. Some of the worst abuses have occurred in this area, which is clearly open to inaccuracy, omission, and half-truth. The stereotyping and blurring of distinctions in a society's attitude toward its minorities would, of course, be duplicated and extended in the textbooks used by that society.

Twenty-one years ago when the American Council on Education studied the treatment of minorities in secondary school textbooks, the results were not altogether happy. In 1961 the Anti-Defamation League published a study, *The Treatment of Minorities in Secondary School Textbooks*, which concluded: "Although there has been marked, but very uneven improvement in intergroup relations content since 1949, only a few books within each subject-area category (i.e., American history, world history, problems of American democracy) give a realistic and constructive portrayal of certain minority groups. No one book gives an adequate presentation of all four topics covered by this report." Similarly, in the current study by Michael Kane, the conclusions are not happy or comforting. Whatever progress has been made in erasing clichés about minority groups has been far less than adequate in light of the rapid social and educational changes of the last two decades. When we consider, for example, the new intense interest of minority groups in their rich pasts and hopeful futures, the improvement seems feeble indeed. Again, the study concludes that not one of the textbooks analyzed is satisfactory with regard to all topics under investigation.

The criteria employed in this study are *objective*— each is applied to the individual text in an identical manner. The application of the criteria, though, is ultimately *subjective,* since, after all, a single individual is making the judgments. A selected passage about, say, slavery, could be objectively analyzed by the criterion of comprehensiveness; yet subjectively the author's appraisal might be affected by his own moral condemnation of slavery. In the end it is up to the reader to make a judgment on his own. It is hoped that the guidelines in this book will help him do precisely that.

Time is a problem in any undertaking of this kind. The author cannot study textbooks up to the day of the publication of his own book; there must be a cut-off point. In this study, however, every publisher was asked to submit updated versions of textbooks scheduled for publication. As a result, though a few 1970 textbooks are dealt with here, the majority of the texts were published before 1970. Some publishers will be releasing revised editions of their books which were not available at the time of the Kane study, but this fact in no way invalidates any of its points. First of all, many months may elapse between the publication date of a revised edition and its purchase and distribution by school systems. It will probably be years before most systems possess new editions. Second, many of the textbooks analyzed are not being revised this year at all. It must be said, too, that the interested observer of secondary school textbooks is obliged to remain skeptical of the extent and depth of any improvements to be made in forthcoming revisions. If past experience is any guide, most book publishers have a long way to go before their revised texts even approach an adequate, accurate treatment of minorities. Mark M. Krug, in the May 1970 *School Review* article referred to by Kane, comes to similar conclusions in regard to textbook treatment of black Americans.

One of the strong points of Kane's study is that it complements its criticisms with recommendations. He feels that educators and organizations should increasingly emphasize the role of minorities in a pluralistic society such as ours in America. The drive for historical accuracy has barely begun, although both printed and audio-visual materials could be utilized to achieve such accuracy.

As well as increasing the historical accuracy of textbooks, school systems must be influenced so they will act as agents of change. This can be accomplished if educators refuse to purchase merely the "best available" text, but insist on needed improvements. One large-city school system has already done this; others must do likewise.

Additionally, educators and organizations should work with civil rights groups to convene a national panel of educators and scholars in order to outline a model text which is historically accurate and substantially relevant for the contemporary student.

Recently educators and others have discussed the desirability of eliminating textbooks as teaching instruments altogether and replacing them with documents and other original source materials. This method, it has been argued, will force students to confront history directly rather than merely absorbing material from condensed summaries of events. This argument surely has some validity. In an age of sophisticated educational techniques, the textbook does occasionally seem inadequate. Nonetheless, the textbook is at present our single vehicle for conveying information. The percentage of students using textbooks, as measured against those who use other materials, is high indeed. It seems therefore that the wisest thing to be done now is to scrutinize carefully existing textbooks and evaluate them from a variety of vantage points. In this way, the realities of the present can be dealt with while other approaches to teaching are simultaneously explored and developed.

If textbooks remain inadequate in certain areas, however, their replacement by other instruments is inevitable. The publication of supplementary materials on intergroup relations topics seems to be a step in the right direction.

The Anti-Defamation League will be involved in various ways with these suggestions and with other conclusions, implicit and explicit, of this study. We believe educators and organizations must become involved if easy stereotypes and blatant inaccuracies are to be eliminated once and for all from contemporary textbooks. Gradualism is insufficient; publishers and authors must be brought to perceive the urgency of the problem. Whether or not the textbook remains as the essential tool in the teaching of social studies and other subjects, the times will no longer allow or tolerate half measures, distortions, or omissions in the teaching of history. If textbooks appreciably improve, all future teaching methods will be the better for it. If textbooks fail to improve rapidly, our knowledge of both the past and the present suffer, and a future of truth and fairness to all groups will be a far dimmer reality than it is at present. Such a state of affairs would be a negative omen for America.

OSCAR COHEN
National Program Director,
Anti-Defamation League of
B'nai B'rith

ACKNOWLEDGMENTS

Although I accept responsibility for the analyses, findings, and opinions in this report, it could not have been written without the support of numerous staff members of the Anti-Defamation League. It was Oscar Cohen, National Director of ADL's Program Division, who recognized the need for such a review, initiated the project, and supported it through each stage of the work. Harold Schiff, Director of Research and Curriculum, generously contributed his efforts and resources in locating data on textbook usage. In addition, his frequent comments and criticisms were useful. The opinions of Walter Plotch, Education Director, were necessary and welcome.

In a project of this type there is often someone in the background whose contributions can never be truly measured or adequately acknowledged. Stan Wexler, Director of Publications, has played such a role in this project. Always available when needed, Mr. Wexler was a ready listener and never failed to provide encouragement and confidence. I doubt whether this report could have been written without our many sessions together. I am grateful for his contributions, and, most important, his friendship.

Of course there remain those personally close whose influence on my judgments and views cannot be properly acknowledged here.

M.B.K.

TABLE OF CONTENTS

INTRODUCTION

. . . The whole world is uneasy. We are in the
midst of an era of tensions, and not the least
among them are tensions among groups in the
American population. Such tensions are serious threats to the American way of life, to
our unity as a people, and to our economic,
political and cultural welfare. Intergroup conflict is far more dangerous than are many of
the more obvious, less insidious external
threats against which we now erect barriers.*

These words are as appropriate today as when
they were written twenty years ago. Their use then
was to introduce the American Council on Education's comprehensive and now classic study, *Intergroup Relations in Teaching Materials.* That study
found textbooks in use throughout the United States
to be distressingly inadequate, inappropriate, and
even damaging to intergroup relations. Eleven years
later, the Anti-Defamation League conducted a similar study to ascertain whether those years had seen
a change in textbook treatment of minorities. The
findings, general and specific, differed little from
those of the 1949 study. That the decade of the
1960's has been one of tensions among groups in
the American population is true. Yet it has also been

---

*Committee on the Study of Teaching Materials in Inter-
group Relations, *Intergroup Relations in Teaching Materials*
(Washington, D.C.: American Council on Education, 1947),
p. 155. (Hereafter cited as A.C.E. Study.)

a decade of increasing recognition for many groups and of increasingly healthy intergroup relations, suggesting that it is time to re-examine those materials from which our young citizens learn about their country and its varied groups. Intergroup conflict *is* far more dangerous than external threats we now confront. To what extent does the material which textbooks present contribute to that conflict? This study is designed to help answer that question.

Just what do current junior and senior high school social studies texts now tell their young readers about Jews? About Nazi persecution of minorities? About black Americans? Or about Americans of Indian, Oriental, or Spanish-speaking backgrounds? Answers to these questions in the past were not encouraging. New and hopefully different ones are now sought. Admittedly, textbooks alone are not sufficient in giving youth a sound education in intergroup relations. However, the 1960 ADL study noted that "as the most universally used teaching tool, what they say, what they imply and what they omit is important."* Textbook publishers and authors must be apprised as to how well they have responded to past criticisms.

Methodology

Forty-five social studies textbooks were chosen for study in this report. Their selection resulted from a survey to ascertain which books, of the multitude of available texts, were used most widely by American schoolchildren. Over fifty localities representing all geographic areas of the United States—ranging

---

*Lloyd Marcus, *The Treatment of Minorities in Secondary School Textbooks* (New York: Anti-Defamation League of B'nai B'rith, 1961). (Hereafter cited as ADL Study.)

from entire states to major cities, to smaller county and city school districts—responded to a request for information on which texts they used most extensively in the teaching of American history, world history, and social problems and civics. From the texts named, forty-five were selected for their ubiquity. The books were equally divided among the subject-matter areas mentioned above: fifteen American histories, fifteen world histories, and fifteen dealing with governmental processes and/or social problems. While the majority of books in each category are designed for use by senior high school classes, some are intended for use in the junior high school. In all cases care was taken to make sure that the edition of the textbook reviewed was the most current then available. Nineteen of the forty-five books here reviewed are later editions of texts examined in the 1960 study. All books selected for analysis are listed in the Appendix.

For the purpose of comparability, this study follows the format established by the 1960 Anti-Defamation League textbook study. That is, it is subdivided by topics as follows:

Section I. Textbook treatment of the Jews. This section reviews the treatment accorded the Jews in textbook material dealing with such topics as ancient Middle Eastern civilizations, the crucifixion, the Middle Ages, colonial and contemporary America. Focusing the study on intergroup relations in the United States does not obviate the need to review historical references to Jews throughout the world. Certainly these references shape the images secondary school youths acquire of their Jewish classmates and other fellow citizens.

Section II. Textbook treatment of minorities under Nazism. The anti-Semitic desecrations which

abounded in many parts of the United States and
Europe in the early months of 1960 prompted the
inclusion of this section in the 1960 study. Its rele-
vancy today is justified by the many incidents of
desecration in the late 1960's. As Dr. Lloyd Marcus
said in 1960:

> Within a world of diverse peoples, it is essen-
> tial that young citizens know what has hap-
> pened when intergroup hostilities have been
> cultivated and exploited to the ultimate degree.
> Textbooks have a definite role to play in as-
> suring that those whose parents [and grand-
> parents] fought totalitarian aggressions in World
> War II do not grow up in ignorance of the
> consequences of racism as an ideology, the
> swastika as a symbol of Hitlerian terror, and
> the evolution and full horror of genocide. These
> aspects of Germany's Third Reich have an im-
> portant bearing on education for citizenship in
> an interreligious, interracial America.*

*Section III. Textbook treatment of black Ameri-
cans.* The 1960's has been a decade of unprecedented action on the part of the largest minority
group in the United States, black Americans. A significant aspect of the civil rights movement has been
its focus on gaining adequate and justified representation of the black American heritage in textbooks
and other classroom materials. This section reviews
the treatment accorded our black population's historical background by textbooks, the current status
of black Americans presented by these books, and
other relevant topics such as race and racial group-
ings.

---

*ADL Study, p. 8.

Section IV. Textbook treatment of other minorities. The black man and the Jew are not the only minority peoples in our population who have been insufficiently represented in our textbooks. This section reviews textbook material on Asiatic minorities in the United States and on our growing Spanish-speaking population, represented especially by the Mexican American and Puerto Rican migrants to the continental United States. A review of historical as well as contemporary material on that onetime majority group, the American Indian, is also included in this section.

In all sections of this report, comparisons are made with the findings of both the 1960 ADL study and the 1949 report of the American Council on Education. In this way the nature of the progress made during the last twenty years in the textbook treatment of minorities can be noted.

Evaluative Criteria

In the 1960 ADL study seven criteria were consistently employed in assessing text material. Studies done by others since 1960 have used some or all of these criteria. Because of their inherent value and proven usefulness, as well as for purposes of comparability, this study has also used those same yardsticks. In the various sections of the study, the seven criteria are referred to by the following key words— or their derivatives:

1. *Inclusion.* Information about Nazi persecution, Negroes, Jews, or other minority groups should be incorporated in all relevant portions of the respective texts.

2. *Validity.* Accurate statements should clearly present the pertinent information; they should never be misleading or ambiguous.

3. *Balance*. All aspects of the subject—both negative and positive—should be given reasonable attention; overemphasis on any one aspect to the neglect of another should be avoided to prevent distorted impressions.

4. *Comprehensiveness*. The range of human characteristics should be described in reference to any or all groups so as to eliminate the danger of stereotyping according to race, religion, or national origin or ancestry. Such matters as cultural assimilation and diverse factors affecting groups should be included where relevant.

5. *Concreteness*. The material should be primarily factual and objective. Generalizations, editorializing, and platitudes should be avoided.

6. *Unity*. Information about each group that is dealt with, at any one time and place, should be sufficiently concentrated to be meaningful rather than fragmented into scattered passing references.

7. *Realism*. Social evils, such as Nazi genocide of minorities and restrictive immigration, and unsolved problems, including prejudice and discrimination, should receive frank treatment rather than being defended, minimized, or ignored.

These criteria were used to judge the adequacy or inadequacy of textbook presentations relevant to each section of this study.

Although quantitative data are presented, a major portion of the study is devoted to actual quotations from the textbooks. It is essential that the textbooks be allowed to speak for themselves, so that the reader too can apply the evaluative criteria to a specific treatment. In all cases every effort is made to ensure that the passages selected are representative of the varying approaches to the topic at hand.

Limitations

Simply put, the intent of this study was to determine *in general* the quality of materials provided by secondary school social studies textbooks on topics related to this nation's major minority groups. The study is *not* designed to be used as an evaluative tool in examining individual textbooks and it must not be taken as such.

In each section many textbooks are quoted, and a book praised in one section may be criticized soundly in another. The object is to demonstrate to the reader what is available on a given topic, not to discuss how a specific book deals with all the topics. The topic is always the focus, not the textbook itself.

Rather than suggesting a model treatment of the topic at hand, this study contrasts the types of treatments given it by the textbooks themselves. In this manner what might be construed as unrealistic suggestions have been avoided. Unfortunately, however, this does not allow us to deal as completely as we would desire with topics which lack adequate treatment. But in these cases the reader himself should be able to suggest many valid ways of handling the topics.

The fact that this study does not analyze the individual textbook, but rather the treatments available on a particular topic, gives rise to another limitation. Many different types of textbooks are dealt with under each topic: American histories, world histories, social problems and civics texts. Individually, these may be designed for use in junior high school, in senior high school, or by "slow," "fast," or "average" students. Although books covering the different subject-matter areas are usually dealt with separately, it is possible that under a given topic a "slow" junior high school civics text may be contrasted with an "advanced" senior high problems text or that some other such combination may exist. It may seem inappropriate to expect the same quantity and style of coverage from two different books written for two different populations of students. However, this study assumes that any topic selected for any textbook should be dealt with in a fashion judged adequate by the criteria of the study. There is no reason why a child in a "slow" junior high school should be presented with a misleading or one-sided treatment of a topic.

The reader may note the type of text being quoted on a particular topic, but he should not let that fact influence the quality he demands from the text. In some cases a particular topic is omitted by a text or a group of texts because it is inappropriate to their subject matter as a whole. However, if the topic *is* included, it must be treated adequately, no matter the type of text it appears in.

In one crucial way, this study differs sharply from that of 1960. In 1960 the texts cited were not identified; the reader did not even know from what type of text an excerpt was taken. But, neither was the reader tempted to use the study as a tool in evaluating individual texts. Today on the other hand, the consumer can make his concern felt, his voice heard. Since the reader of this study is concerned with what students are being offered, he should be alerted as to how a particular text handles a given topic. For that reason the sources of all quotes are identified.

However, the reader is cautioned once again to realize that evaluation of a specific textbook's treatment of a topic or portion of a topic is not meant to be an evaluation of the textbook as a whole. Even the best of the books reviewed fell short of meeting the criteria for all the topics examined. Hence each excerpt should be considered as but one piece of information about that particular book, regardless of whether the quotation elicited praise or condemnation. In most cases the thoughtful reader needs more than the information presented here to judge the worth of a specific text, but our data should enable him to examine the texts his children or students use, and to form an evaluation of them. Taken in its entirety, the information in this report does provide a representative picture of wherein textbooks may succeed or fail.

In summary, this report is a general statement of how textbooks deal with the many minority groups in this nation and of what types of information they offer their readers about these groups. It was undertaken to determine how textbook treatments of these groups have changed over the past decade. The findings indicate that a follow-up study which offers a precise content analysis of individual texts is in order.

As was found in the previous ADL study, for each of the major topics reviewed the available text material ranged from that which was accurate, complete, and of value in improving intergroup relations to that which was misleading, one-sided, and prejudicial. Within the latter group many books ignored a given topic entirely. The 1960 study was able to report "marked, if uneven, improvement in textbook treatment of intergroup relations since 1949."* Unfortunately the same evaluation applies to the findings of the current study. There has been "marked, if uneven," progress in certain areas, but on the

---

*ADL Study, p. 10.

whole textbook material concerning minority groups in the United States must still be considered inadequate. As was the case with the 1960 study, no one textbook, regardless of how inspired its treatment of any single subject may be, has been found which by itself presents a reasonably complete and undistorted picture of the many minority groups in America. The unsuitability of any textbook as a source of intergroup knowledge for a social studies class prompts the repetition of these observations from the 1960 study:

> In specific areas of concern, a large number of America's most widely used social studies textbooks have startling omissions and other gross inadequacies. Thus, the danger of relying on texts—and especially on one rather than several texts—as the sole form of instructional material becomes evident.
>
> Development of critical thinking requires the gathering and analysis of all pertinent facts for relative validity in order that sound conclusions may be drawn. Development of competence for participation in a democratic society demands balanced, rounded knowledge of the nature of the people and their problems in a pluralistic nation, as well as an understanding of, and dedication to, the principles set forth in the Bill of Rights. No one text can achieve these ends; many books and many other printed and audio-visual materials are needed.*

Textbooks alone are not sufficient if better intergroup understanding is a goal to be met in schools

---

*ADL Study, p. 10.

and by social studies classes in particular. It is the teacher, not the textbook, that will make the difference in the classroom. The text is merely a tool and, as this report indicates, quite possibly an inadequate one at best. It is the teacher's scholarship, integrity, and creativity that will determine how effectively a text will be used. A teacher who is aware of the shortcomings of his tools can compensate by bringing in other resources. Even the worst text can be used by the teacher to offer his students a lesson in concealed prejudice, poor generalizations, and illogical reasoning.

It is our hope that this report will alert more teachers and parents to the inadequacies that exist in the textbooks provided for today's schoolchildren.

CHAPTER ONE

TEXTBOOK TREATMENT OF THE JEWS

The 1949 Report of the A.C.E.'s Committee on the Study of Teaching Materials in Intergroup Relations revealed that the characteristics, history, and problems of Jews were inadequately presented in the textbooks studied. Specifically the committee found the following:

A. Material about Jews dealt mainly with the period before A.D. 79. Students received the impression that little had happened to Jews and Judaism since then and that today's Jews were, in fact, a remnant of a past civilization.

B. The crucifixion story was presented so sketchily that anti-Jewish feelings of pupils could well be reinforced.

C. Material on Jews in medieval and modern Europe was inadequate and dealt mostly with persecution, not with their contributions or their constructive relationships with other people. (A.C.E. did not, of course, cover material on Israel. However, the 1960 ADL study and this study do review accounts of this topic.)

D. Material presented on American Jews was inaccurate. There was little to show the many differences among Jewish subgroups and individuals in the United States. Common stereotypes of Jews were not challenged.

E. Jews were sometimes referred to as a "race."

These criticisms, with the exception of the last

item, held true for many of the textbooks reviewed by the 1960 ADL study, *The Treatment of Minorities in Secondary School Textbooks*. Now, a full twenty years since the criticisms were first voiced, they are still applicable to many of the secondary school social studies texts used in our nation's classrooms. The textbook portrayal of the Jews in history and in contemporary American life is woefully inadequate as measured by either quality or quantity of reference. Since the original criticisms apply, the findings of the present study will be summarized within their framework.

A. THE JEWS AS A REMNANT OF A PAST CIVILIZATION

World history textbooks continue to follow the practice of devoting much more space to the ancient Hebrews than to later Jewish history. Some still fail, in places, to distinguish between the ancient Hebrews and the Jews of later times. As this failure contributes to a conception of the Jews as an unchanging, separate, ingrown people, the texts fail to meet the criterion of *validity* and contribute to reinforcing the stereotypes that handicap successful intergroup relations. For these reasons the passages below fall short of achieving *balance* and *comprehensiveness* in their references to the Jews:

> The great duty of all Hebrews has been to obey the law of the God Jehovah, which states what is right and wrong—their moral code. Their duty has also been to obey the commandments about living together as a tribal people. (*Our Widening World*)

> When the Persians captured Babylon, their king, Cyrus, freed the Hebrews and allowed them to go home to Jerusalem. Since then, like

Egypt and Mesopotamia, Palestine has been ruled by several empires. The Hebrews have been scattered all over the world, and persecution has been their lot. Yet many have held staunchly to their faith. For centuries they looked toward establishing in Palestine an independent Hebrew nation. In 1948 their dream came true. (*Our World Through the Ages*)

While direct efforts to overcome the stereotype of the Jew as a remnant of an ancient civilization are not made by any of the textbooks examined, the treatment accorded the ancient Hebrews has been found to be *comprehensive* and *balanced* in a greater percentage of the books reviewed than it had been in the past. In 1960 fewer than half of the world history books linked the traditions of the ancient Hebrews to modern times and the moral values of today. Currently twelve of the fifteen world history texts studied make such a connection. The examples below demonstrate how effectively a social studies text can contribute to a student's understanding of, and respect for, the heritage of his Jewish companions.

Because of its emphasis on ethics (proper conduct), the Jewish form of monotheism is often called ethical monotheism. It is the supreme gift of the Hebrews to Western civilization. It is not an invention or a discovery to make life easier. It is a great and noble idea; and ideas, as you know, are powerful. No other single idea has so profoundly influenced Western civilization. (*Men and Nations*)

The Hebrews . . . believed that there is one God of the whole universe, and that belief has become a part of our own culture. (*A History of the World*)

The Hebrews' contribution to world cultures was spiritual. Their religious teachings have outlived the material riches acquired by ancient empires and remain as a powerful influence on mankind. (*World History and Cultures: The Story of Man's Achievements*)

The Hebrew gift to civilization was not in material wealth, that is, they are not known for their elaborate buildings or luxurious palaces. They developed the idea of a single God whom they worshiped in simple ways. This belief was different from the practice of polytheism in other nations of that time. The holy writings of the Hebrews included the Ten Commandments and the Old Testament. Unlike other religions, the Hebrew faith stressed a belief in the brotherhood of man, taught the importance of peace, and pleaded for a moral society based on laws. (*The Pageant of World History*)

As in the last example cited, most world history texts indicate that the Old Testament of the Bible was a creation of the ancient Hebrews. Two especially fine examples of this practice are cited below:

The ancient Hebrews had no great armies, never built a vast empire, and made no great contributions in art or science. Their lasting achievement was in the sphere of religion. . . .

The writings [of the prophets] were added to earlier laws and books of sacred history and to favorite stories, proverbs, and inspiring songs of worship. The whole collection

is known as the Old Testament of the Bible.
. . . Its power and beauty . . . have not been
surpassed in any age or language. The ideals
of these desert peoples have become a part of
the heritage of millions in the Western world.
(*New Dimensions of World History*)

The Old Testament is a collection of Israelite literature. The experiences of the ancient
Israelites are recorded in 39 "books" in that
part of the Bible which is called the Old Testament. There you find the Israelite story of
the creation of the world, the Ten Commandments, and the other Laws of Moses. In it also
are stories, poems, and wise sayings called
proverbs. Some of the "books" deal with the
history of the Israelites; others are the teachings of the prophets.

This collection of Hebrew writings not only
is one of our finest inheritances from the past
but has had tremendous influence on our modern world. Jews accept it as their sacred Scrip-
ture, while Christians look upon the Old
Testament as the foundation for the teachings
of Jesus. (*The History of Our World*)

Beyond merely identifying the ancient Hebrews'
contributions to the Bible, a few texts quite directly
credit them with providing the foundations for other
major world religions. This is typified by such passages as "Judaism formed the base of two other
great religions of the world—Christianity and Is-
lam" (*Living World History*), and "From this faith
[in God] stemmed at least [because the followers of
Mohammed also accept some of the religious beliefs of the Hebrews] two great religions, Judaism
and Christianity" (*The History of Our World*).

Other textbooks indicate the Jewish origins of Christianity by identifying Jesus and his disciples as Jews. This approach is represented in a selection which states that "The Hebrews also gave Christianity to the world through the life and teachings of Jesus" (*The Record of Mankind*). Or consider these rather inclusive descriptions of Jesus and early Christianity:

> There [in Nazareth] he [sic] worked as a carpenter and, like all Jewish boys, studied the writings of the Hebrew prophets. In his studies, he displayed a keen interest and aptitude for Jewish religious teachings." (*Story of Nations*)

> During the lifetime of Jesus and immediately after his crucifixion, all Christians were Jewish. But Paul, a Hellenized Jew who lived in the city of Tarsus in Asia Minor, boldly denied that Jesus was sent merely as the redeemer of the Jews. A loving Father had sent His only Son to atone for the sins of all mankind. Therefore Christianity was not a sect of Judaism. It was a new church, a church for Gentiles as well as for Jews. Paul's approach meant that Christianity henceforth could appeal not only to a handful of Jews, but to the millions of Gentiles who made up most of the population of the Roman Empire. (*A Global History of Man*)

Still other world history texts demonstrate the link between the ancient Hebrews and modern democratic thought by references to the Judaeo-Christian tradition:

The most ancient Hebrew prophets and the first Christians preached the doctrine of the brotherhood of man. Both groups stressed respect for the dignity of every individual and concern for "the poor and disinherited." Thus the spirit of democracy existed long ago in the Jewish-Christian tradition. (*Our World Through the Ages*)

Democracy is only one of the many ideals which have come to you from across the years. Your standards of right and wrong have been developed largely from the ideals of the Hebrews and the Christians. The Ten Commandments of the Hebrew Old Testament have been written into the laws under which you live. And the ancient Christian teaching to "love thy neighbor as thyself" expresses an ideal that is very much alive in your world. (*A History of the World*)

However enlightened the references quoted in this section may be, it must be realized that not all world history textbooks used in our schools are as *comprehensive* or well *balanced* in their portrayal of the ancient Hebrews. Christianity's Jewish origins and our culture's legacy of ethical and democratic values from the Hebrews are not always subjects of *inclusion*. In only one instance the ancient Hebrews were mentioned in a text other than a world history. A civics text acknowledged the contributions of the ancient Hebrews to today's governmental concepts:

In ancient Hebrew civilization some elements of modern citizenship began to appear. The Hebrew was a subject of his king, to whom he owed loyalty and obedience. But in the He-

send even more troops into the country. They looked for a way to discredit Jesus. One of the disciples of Jesus, called Judas, offered to betray his master for thirty pieces of silver. Jesus was quickly taken prisoner and hailed before the Roman governor, Pontius Pilate (*pahn-shus py-lut*), for judgment. Jesus was charged with stirring up the people and attempting to set himself up as a king in opposition to the Romans. Pilate could find no proof of the charges, and, fearing a riot, offered to set Jesus free. The crowd that had gathered for the trial protested. Many of those present were enemies of Jesus and they began to demand his death. Pilate did not wish to anger the crowd and perhaps provoke demonstrations among the large numbers of Jewish pilgrims who were crowding into Jerusalem for the holy days. He sentenced the prisoner to death by crucifixion, or execution by being nailed to a wooden cross, and had the sentence carried out." (*Story of Nations*)

Three other texts are less direct in linking the Jews with the actual condemnation of Jesus. However, they serve only to intensify the confusion surrounding the circumstances of Jesus' death:

Although Jesus often said that the body of law which God had given to the Jews through Moses was not to be done away with, it seemed to many that Jesus was breaking that law. They were shocked by the claim that Jesus was the son of God. Jesus was denounced to the Roman governor, Pontius Pilate, as a blasphemer. He was condemned to die and was put to death on the cross, the method used by the Romans for executing common criminals. (*New Dimensions of World History*)

At about the age of thirty-three, Jesus encountered the serious opposition of Jewish religious leaders in Jerusalem. They rejected the idea of some of his followers that Jesus was the Messiah (the Saviour whose coming had been predicted by the ancient prophets). He was denounced for blasphemy and charged with wanting to become king of the Jews. He was turned over to the Roman governor, Pontius Pilate.

Jesus was accused of causing unrest and of challenging Roman authority. Condemned to death, Jesus was crucified on a great wooden cross. (*A World History: A Cultural Approach*)

But some people in Palestine regarded Jesus as a religious troublemaker, while others were disappointed that he would not lead a revolt against the Romans. So enemies of Jesus turned him over to Pontius Pilate (*pahn' shus pie'lut*), the Roman governor of Palestine. Pilate, who perhaps thought religious unrest might lead to political disturbances, permitted Jesus to be put to death. (*The History of Our World*)

All the above accounts handle the crucifixion in a way that is somewhat misleading and easily subject to misinterpretation. To the extent that this is so in the individual case, that text must be faulted on the criteria of *validity, balance,* and *concreteness.*

Only one text can be singled out for mentioning both Jewish and Roman opposition to Jesus while not implicating the Jews in the actual circumstances of his death:

> When he traveled to Jerusalem in about 30 A.D., many Jews there hailed him as the Messiah and as "King of the Jews." Others, however—especially the conservative priestly class of Jews—denied that he was the Messiah and opposed this claim.
>
> The Romans feared that Jesus wanted to lead an uprising and regarded him as an enemy of the state. Jesus was tried before a Roman court and executed by crucifixion—a common Roman punishment at that time. (*Men and Nations*)

Of the four other texts that deal with the crucifixion story, three mention only the Romans in this connection and the fourth merely states that "Jesus died on the cross on a hill near Jerusalem about the year A.D. 29" (*The Record of Mankind*).

Dr. Lloyd Marcus stated in 1960 that:

> Specialists in intergroup relations have long contended that world history texts could do much to counteract the "Christ-killer" concept in anti-Semitism by including fuller, more factual presentations of the events leading to the Crucifixion, with particular attention to forces at work throughout the Holy Land at that time which led many people to desire the removal of any "messiah." No textbook was found which provides such a rounded, comprehensive account.*

Today, a decade later, that still necessary text-

---

*ADL Study, p. 14.

book has not been provided to our students and their teachers. At the least, one would expect texts to be more frank about the actual lack of scholarly evidence concerning the specific events during the last days of Jesus. But still to have texts in the classroom that unequivocally or even subtly point the finger of blame at the Jews is an affront to rational men of all religious and scholarly persuasions.

C. JEWS IN MEDIEVAL AND MODERN EUROPE: A HISTORY OF PERSECUTION

That Jews existed in Europe between the crucifixion and the rise of Hitler is a fact completely overlooked by four of the fifteen world history books currently reviewed. And those histories that mention the Jews at all continue to place the major, if not sole, emphasis on persecution, isolation, and exile. There is only one noteworthy exception to this practice. In a rambling account, this text demonstrates how the criteria of *inclusion, balance, comprehensiveness,* and *unity* can be met in outlining the place of the Jews in a comprehensive history of our world:

> By the end of the Hellenistic Age, Jews were dispersed throughout the Roman Empire. They settled in Europe and the Mediterranean lands, in the *Diaspora,* which means "dispersion" and refers to all lands in which they were scattered. Often, in the medieval and modern period, Jews suffered from discriminatory laws that prohibited them from engaging in certain occupations, limited the places where they would live, and denied them citizenship. This discrimination is usually referred to as *anti-Semitism.* The darkest chapter of Jewish history was written in Hitler's Ger-

many, where six million European Jews were killed outright or tortured to death in concentration camps operated by the Nazis. The Jew has, indeed, sampled beyond measure, man's inhumanity to man.

Yet, the Jews and Judaism have enjoyed a remarkable record of religious creativity. The idea of a Messianic Age with the establishment of the Kingdom of God on earth, prayer, the observation of the Sabbath, and study as a religious obligation—all these sustained them. The institution of the synagogue, the ministry of spiritual leadership of the rabbi, and the Bible with the Oral Law kept the Jews loyal to their tradition.

The Jewish love of learning produced a long continuous chain of scholars and thinkers. There was Philo of Alexandria, who first struggled to bring Greek and Hebrew thought together, and Saadia Gaon, a Babylonian who wrote of reason and revelation. In the eleventh century, Rabbi Solomon ben Isaac of France wrote a commentary on the Talmud and the Bible that is still used today. Moses Maimonides, physician to the Sultan of Cairo in the twelfth century, attempted to reconcile Judaism with Aristotle's philosophy. The Jews were a cultural bridge between the Arabs who continued Greek ideas and medieval Christendom.

The Jews have played an important role in man's struggle for freedom and enlightenment. Out of their long historical experience as a minority, they learned to treasure freedom, and with their great cultural heritage, they made important contributions wherever they went. The contributions to the modern world by Jewish scholars, writers, and scientists like Spinoza, Freud, Einstein, and many others have been immense. (*Man's Cultural Heritage*)

In contrast, the only other extensive account of the Jews primarily emphasizes the persecution they suffered at the hands of various European rulers and peoples:

> During medieval times many Jews lived in Europe, northern Africa, and western Asia, but as Christianity became dominant intolerant leaders persecuted them. In many countries Christians were forbidden to live among the Jews, thus forcing the latter to live in areas of their own called *ghettos*. But long before this, Jews in some countries could not own land, farm, join a labor guild, or enter most of the professions. These injustices caused many Jews to become merchants or moneylenders. Church laws which forbade Christians to lend money at interest did not, of course, apply to the Jews. For centuries they were the bankers of Europe.
>
> The political and financial policies of some kings resulted in the Jews of Europe being persecuted and then in being driven out of England (1290), France (1306), Spain (1492), and Portugal (1496). They fled to Poland, Turkey and other Moslem lands, and to the Americas.
>
> Here and there the Jews were able to build synagogues and be instructed by learned rabbis. Their religious leaders continued to write commentaries on religion and philosophy and

keep old traditions alive. Some of their brightest days occurred in Spain in the eighth and ninth centuries. Some of the best writing of the time in philosophy, medicine, science, and mathematics was accomplished by Spanish Jews in this period of comparative tolerance. (*World History and Cultures: The Story of Man's Achievements*)

The only frequent mention of Jews in medieval Europe is in connection with the fifteenth-century expulsion from Spain. Five of the seven texts that include the event portray the Jews positively and point out what Spain lost by exiling these people. One text states that Spain lagged behind other European nations because "the Moors and Jews, who had once formed an enterprising middle class, had been expelled in the late 1400's" (*Men and Nations*). Another reads: "Actually this policy [religious intolerance] hurt Spain economically by robbing it of its most skilled merchants and manufacturers" (*Our World Through the Ages*). A third points out that ". . . people such as the Moors and Jews who might have helped Spain become rich were persecuted and driven out. Soon Spain, once a leading country of Europe, took second place in the commercial and political affairs of Europe" (*The Pageant of World History*).

From the Spanish inquisitions up to the establishment of the state of Israel only the briefest, most perfunctory statements are made concerning the Jews. Universally these deal with either the granting or restriction of political or civil rights under eighteenth- and nineteenth-century European rulers in Austria, France, England, or Russia. It is only with the treatment of modern Israel that we get a picture of Jews as real people—people with feelings and abilities, people with occupations and families, people with dreams and ambitions, people who for once are pictured as individuals rather than as a collectivity.

D. THE ESTABLISHMENT AND SURVIVAL OF ISRAEL

Of the sixteen world history texts reviewed in 1960, only eight offered adequate coverage of Israel as measured by the criteria of the study. Currently, eleven of the fifteen world histories examined supply accounts that meet these criteria. In addition, one social problems text and two American histories offer satisfactory accounts. Of those world histories that fall short of the standards, three lacked either *balance,* or *comprehensiveness,* or *unity,* or a combination of the three. The fourth was simply too superficial to meet even the criteria of *inclusion.* Those texts found to lack *balance* or *comprehensiveness* tell only of the problems of Israel and do not refer to her advances. These accounts stand out in stark contrast to some of the six-to-ten-page discussions available which tell of Israel's birth in the minds of a few, its gradual evolution to nationhood, and its dramatic political and economic gains. As an example, compare the difference in *balance* evidenced by the second passage below in dealing with the same subject as the first:

> To make matters worse, Israel has promised to allow any Jew who wishes to do so to make his home in Israel. The Jews come from many parts of the world. They are usually very poor, they do not speak Hebrew and, some can neither read nor write. They do not have the skills for farm or factory that Israel needs.

They must be housed, fed, and clothed until they can care for themselves. All this makes it difficult for a new nation. (*The Pageant of World History*).

Some Unique Domestic Problems of Israel. Israel is a tiny country with a population of more than 2,500,000. Yet it has promised to admit any Jews, even paupers, wishing to go there. Immigrants have come to Israel from practically every country. Even though they are Jews, their backgrounds, languages, and customs are so different that they often scarcely understand one another. In general, the earlier immigrants were highly educated, often professional people from Western Europe. In general, the later immigrants have been underprivileged people, with little educational background, from North Africa and Asia. (*Our World Through the Ages*)

Happily, the latter passage is indicative of the constructive treatment given Israel and the Jews by most world history texts. Students are frequently told of how "in gratitude [to Chaim Weizmann], and to secure Jewish support for the Allies, the British diplomat Arthur Balfour told Zionist leaders that the British would 'view with favor' the creation of a Jewish 'national home' in Palestine" (*Men and Nations*). The claims of both the Arabs and the Jews on Palestine are discussed frankly, as in the following passages:

The Jews declared that they had a right to a homeland in Palestine because their ancestors had inhabited the land in ancient times, and because there was a need for a land where

Jews could assemble, live without persecution, and preserve their culture. . . .

The Arabs bitterly opposed Zionism and protested that Palestine had been artificially separated from Syria. They pointed out that Arabs had occupied Palestine for hundreds of years and made up the overwhelming majority of its population. They claimed that the establishment of a Jewish state would deprive Arabs of their land and interfere with the geographic and cultural unity of the Arab world. (*A World History: A Cultural Approach*)

The Arabs particularly feared and resented the coming of Jews in numbers. During many centuries the Jews had been separated from this land, and the Arabs had become the great majority. They held this land by the right of their centuries of toil and ownership and they looked upon the Jews as invaders who must be cast out with violence if necessary. The Jews regarded this land as rightfully theirs, for their ancestors had been forcibly removed from it. The Jews believed that the Arabs possessed a land not theirs by ancient right. These peoples were determined to maintain their just claims, and there began a history of violence which stained the land with blood and misery. This controversy continues to torture the relations between the Israeli Jews and their Arab neighbors. (*Man's Cultural Heritage*)

Nor can the political and economic considerations of the day be neglected:

With the Jewish survivors of nazism strewn across Europe in refugee camps, a wrenching

challenge to the world's conscience, Zionist
leaders pressed the British government to
abandon all previous restrictions on immigration into Palestine. The British who had governed Palestine since 1922 as a League of
Nations mandate hesitated to offend the Arab
world. There were important interests to protect, particularly in regard to the oil deposits in
certain Arab lands. (*New Dimensions of
World History*)

No matter how great the problems discussed,
however, the student is not left with the impression
that they are insurmountable. He is shown how "In
agriculture, for example, the Israelis grow several
crops instead of depending on one as is the case in
many parts of the Middle East"; how "Whatever
they do, they use much machinery and modern scientific techniques"; and how this is important for
"the fact that the Israeli farmers can enjoy a reasonable standard of living is a great boost for their national industry. Since the farmers can afford to buy
something more than bare essentials, Israeli industry has a flourishing domestic market." (*A Global
History of Man*)

Texts discuss the three wars of survival the Israelis have been engaged in, often with outright praise
for their military abilities. Photographs of Israeli
farms, cities, soldiers, and industrial enterprises are
found in many of the texts examined.

In their treatment of modern Israel those responsible for the contents of world history textbooks have
shown that the Jews need not be treated as a static
remnant of an ancient civilization. The passage below exemplifies how Jews have been shown to be a

modern, dynamic people contributing to their betterment and providing examples for others:

> During the 1950's and 1960's, Israel became a factor in world politics. The Arab states remained determined to destroy the new country. By using the skills brought from Europe by Jewish refugees, by wise capital investment, and by applying the strong nationalistic spirit of the desire for a Jewish homeland, the Jews made Israel into a prosperous modern country of more than two and a half million people. Here, alone in the Middle East, the standard of living approaches that of Europe. Educational facilities are as good as those in developed countries, and democratic political institutions have worked well in an atmosphere of stability and progress. (*The Human Achievement*)

World history texts are offering adequate coverage of Israel. What remains to be done is for more of the many American history and social problems texts that cover the situation in the Middle East to offer accounts as *comprehensive* as the following found in a social problems text:

> There is the possibility that hatred of the Jewish people will unite the Arabs in a "holy war" against Israel. This is becoming more unlikely, since such a conflict could spread into a full-scale global war. Arab hatred of Israel is built on a sense of injustice and revenge. They look upon Israel as part of Arab Palestine, which was in existence for 1,300 years. The Jews look upon Palestine as the one true home of the Jews since Abraham. They think of Is-

rael as the oldest sovereign state in the world, and maintain that it did not lose its franchise when Titus destroyed Jerusalem in A.D. 70.

Shortly after the end of World War I, the Jews began to buy back the land peacefully, purchasing it from the Arab landlords and rebuilding the soil into productive farmland. In May, 1948, when the British mandate over Palestine ended, Israel declared its independence. The new nation was attacked immediately by five Arab nations. The Arabs were repulsed, and the Jews now claim that Israel is theirs by right of conquest.

This incident created a refugee problem. Some 652,000 refugees left Israel, not because they were driven out by the Israeli armies, but because they were ordered out by Arab leaders. The Jews claim that those who left have nursed their hatred for a decade and a half and can no longer be rehabilitated in Israel. Those Arabs who stayed in Israel became citizens and enjoy equal rights with the Jews. (*The Challenge of Democracy*)

E. JEWISH LIFE IN AMERICA

In 1960 textbooks devoted only a distressingly inadequate amount of discussion to Jews and the Jewish heritage in America. Since that time neither the quality nor the quantity of textbook references to the American Jewish people has improved significantly. In fact, one of the fifteen American history texts reviewed does not even attempt to meet the criterion of *inclusion* by mentioning the presence of Jews in America; in the fourteen that do, the references are all too often made in listing the various groups who came to America in colonial days or during one of the great periods of immigration. Actually only two American history texts referred to Jews in contemporary American life:

> *Kennedy's appointments.* The President's Cabinet showed how democratic practices had spread in the postwar years. For example, Kennedy chose as members of his official family two men of Jewish birth—Arthur J. Goldberg and Abraham A. Ribicoff. (Earlier Oscar Straus had served under Theodore Roosevelt, Henry Morgenthau, Jr., under F.D.R., and Lewis L. Strauss under Eisenhower.) (*The Free and the Brave*)

> Roman Catholics and Jews suffered far less from discrimination than in the past. Leaders from these faiths carried on dialogues with each other and with Protestant clergymen. The efforts of Popes John XXIII and Paul VI to bring the Roman Catholic Church up to date led to these dialogues. Neither anti-Catholicism nor anti-Semitism had entirely disappeared, yet never before had there been so cordial a relationship among the Protestant, Roman Catholic, and Jewish religious leaders as in the 1960's (*United States History*)

As indicated above, most of the American history textbook references to Jews in America are entirely too superficial to be considered as meeting the criteria of *inclusion* or *comprehensiveness*. Social problems and civics texts are even weaker in this area. Four of these texts made no mention whatever of Jews. (In 1960 only one of sixteen social problems texts omitted Jews.) Of the eleven remaining texts, ten do no more than matter-of-factly make references to Jewish people in America. They do this typically by reviewing the major religious groups, by showing pictures of a synagogue, or by listing past immigrant groups. As an example of the inadequacy of the texts, consider the passage below. Although this is one of the most extensive references to Jews that can be found in those texts, it hardly meets the dual criteria of *balance* and *comprehensiveness:*

> Over the years Jews have experienced persecution in many lands, nor have they been free from mistreatment in the United States. Anti-Semitic groups—organizations that hate the Jews and seek to persecute them—have existed in America. In the 1920's especially, hostility toward the Jews was an important element in the program of the Ku Klux Klan. Jews have experienced discrimination in employment, in schools, in social organizations, and at resorts. (*Problems of Democracy*)

By contrast, the only social problems text that can be considered adequate on the topic, as measured by the criteria of this study, offered the student more complete background information on the topic of anti-Semitism, but as a part of its discussion of the Jews.

> In 1654 the first group of Jews, 23 citizens from Holland, settled in New Amsterdam. They migrated to America to find freedom and to escape persecution.
> The Jews had been forbidden to own land in Europe. They were harassed with restrictions established by the Inquisitions of Spain and Portugal. Some were thrown into prison and burned at the stake. In many European

cities Jews were confined to the *ghetto,* a section enclosed by a high wall where they were locked up each night. The Jews served as a whipping boy for centuries.

Anti-Semitic propaganda was abetted by the publishing in 1905 of a notorious forgery called *Protocols of the Learned Elders of Zion.* This document purported to show that leading Jews had hatched an international conspiracy to gain control of the finances of the world, thereby enabling them to control all governments. This "document" has since been exposed as a fraud written to incite Russian peasants against the Jews. Whenever a political crisis threatened the government in Czarist Russia, the secret police instigated anti-Jewish pogroms. In the late eighteenth century Russian Jews were exiled to Poland, to White Russia, and to the Ukraine.

Anti-Semitism has also manifested itself in various ways in our country. Social and economic discrimination against Jews is frequently displayed by individuals, hotels, clubs, resorts, and business firms. In some instances Jews are not permitted to join college fraternities and sororities. And the quota system prevents many of them from entering private schools, colleges, and professional schools. The Anti-Defamation League of B'nai B'rith attempts to fight discrimination and anti-Semitism. (*The Challenge of Democracy*)

Whereas most American history references are not quite so incidental as those found in social problems texts, they are far from adequate and certainly do not contribute to better intergroup understanding. Some of the more extensive passages to be found follow:

> *The first Jews.* In September, 1654, New Amsterdam was the scene of the arrival of twenty-three Jews from Brazil. Already tragic wanderers looking for a permanent home, they had originally come from Portugal. Received in New Netherland with only a lukewarm welcome, they gradually found acceptance. They had no idea that they were founding what would become the largest, most influential Jewish community in the world. (*The Adventure of the American People*)

> Because the "new" immigrants were seemingly so different in language, political background, and social customs, the older Americans began to wonder whether they could ever be assimilated (absorbed) into the mainstream of national life. The "new" immigrants were usually poor, and often (except for the Jews) unable to read and write even their native language. They settled together in slums or "ghettoes" in the cities, in "little Italys," "little Polands," and so on. Here they clung to their own familiar language and customs. (*Our American Republic*)

> In addition, a number of European Jews came to America in these decades. They generally settled in cities, where they worked as peddlers, merchants, clothing-manufacturers, teachers, and physicians. Some West Indian Jews of Spanish-Portuguese ancestry emigrated to southern cities. One of them, Judah P. Benjamin of New Orleans, was twice elected to the

United States Senate. (*A History of the United States*)

Religious hostility was also aimed at the Jewish immigrants from eastern Europe. Though Jews had lived in this country from its earliest days, they did not arrive in large numbers until the late 1800's. Because their customs were unfamiliar to many native-born Americans, the Jews encountered much prejudice in the new country. (*A History of the United States*)

As can be seen, these passages hardly offer a *balanced* and *comprehensive* portrait of American Jewry. The 1949 A.C.E. report emphasized that "There are five million Jews in the American population. They are widely distributed in occupation, ability, economic status, and geographical location. So great is the variation among them that there is no typical Jew; that cardinal fact should be emphasized again and again."* However, twenty years later that fact is still not emphasized. Only one of the fifteen American history texts examined can be characterized as adequate in this respect. That text offers the following passage on a page headed by a picture of Touro Synagogue and a rather *concrete* caption explaining its place in the American heritage:

The Jews in America. Many of the immigrants who came from eastern Europe after 1890 were Jews who had fled from Russia. For hundreds of years, Jews had no homeland but were scattered about in small groups in many countries. Because they were persecuted from time

---

*A.C.E. Study, p. 99.

to time in one country or another, Jews have
come to America since its earliest days.

The first Jews, in fact, came before the
American Revolution. Some sought religious
freedom in colonial times in Rhode Island.
During the Revolutionary War, Haym Salomon, a Jewish banker of Philadelphia, raised
large sums of money (much of which came
from his own fortune) to aid the fight for independence. Jewish immigrants came in larger
numbers in the late 1800's and early 1900's.
Most of them settled in cities. They became
doctors, lawyers, or businessmen, or enriched
America's art, literature, music and theater.

The Jews who have come to America do
not represent a separate race or a particular
nation. Throughout centuries of persecution
they were held together by their steadfast
loyalty to the ancient Hebrew religion. (*This
Is America's Story*)

Not concluding simply with the above, the text
goes on to quote the following excerpts from *One
America* (Francis J. Brown and Joseph S. Roucek,
editors):

The Jews as a group by no means form a . . .
unique segment of the American population.
. . . Their callings are as diverse as those of
their fellow Americans. There are rich Jews,
just as there are rich non-Jews. And there are
just as many poor Jews, relatively, as there are
poor non-Jews. Far from being a homogeneous
[uniform] group, the American Jews are . . .
individuals among whom one can find conservatives as well as progressives, Republicans
as well as Democrats, employers as well as em-

ployees, shopkeepers as well as factory workers. In their opinions, attitudes, and political
leanings they differ as much among themselves as do Americans in general. (*This Is
America's Story*)

The only other passage that directly attempts to
dispel the stereotype of Jews as a uniform group is
found in the social problems text singled out for
mention earlier:

It is not true, as generally believed, that Jews
control any particular segment of American
business. The editors of *Fortune* magazine
studied Jewish participation in many fields.
They report that Jewish influence is very small
in automobile manufacturing, steel, rubber,
coal, oil, public utilities, shipping, transporta-
tion, and communications. Two leading five-
and-tens are owned by Woolworth and Kresge,
both non-Jews. Jews are represented in only a
small way in brokerage and insurance. Three
of the eight principal movie concerns are
owned by Jews, but here the management is
divided. Only one-half of 1 percent of the
95,000 bankers in America are Jews, and Jews
own less than 1 percent of our daily newspapers. Most of the American Jews are wage
earners. (*The Challenge of Democracy*)

Another approach to presenting the true diversity
among Americans of Jewish faith or descent is to
single out for identification individual Jewish con-
tributors to American life and history. However, as
the A.C.E. report indicates, "indiscriminate identification of this sort" is not good, "rather it seems
likely to intensify the out-group concept." They rec-
ommend that "identification of an individual with

a group is desirable only when his group membership is pertinent to the point under discussion."*

Three American histories do this by the following means:

A caption to a photograph reads. "Throughout the history of America, immigrants have made invaluable contributions to this country. Austrian-born I. I. Rabi (left) was one of many Jews who came to America. In 1944 he won the Nobel Prize in physics" (*Our American Nation*).

On a page headed "America has drawn its strength from people of varied backgrounds" is a sketch of Haym Salomon accompanied by this caption: "A Jewish merchant and banker, HAYM SALOMON, was forced to flee from Poland for his part in a struggle for Polish freedom. During the American Revolution, he devoted much of his fortune to the Patriot cause" (*This Is America's Story*). The student is then referred to a fuller account of Salomon's life in a section separate from the main body of the text.

A biographical sketch of Haym Salomon, separate from the main text, begins: "Many of those who work hardest for freedom do so because they know from experience what life is like without it. Such was the case with Haym Salomon (1740?–1785). A Jew of Portuguese descent, he was raised in Poland, a land that was partitioned to death by Europe's autocratic rulers. Salomon took part in an unsuccessful Polish struggle for freedom and migrated to New York in 1772. He quickly became a colonial sympathizer in the fight for American independence" (*A History of the United States*).

The social problems text quoted twice before in-

---

*A.C.E. Study, p. 105.

cludes the following under its section headed "The Jews":

> Jews have distinguished themselves in business, the professions, and the field of entertainment. They have also rendered outstanding service to our country. Professor Albert Michelson was a Nobel Prize winner in physics. Dr. Simon Flexner was formerly director of the Rockefeller Institute laboratories; his brother, Abraham Flexner, was noted in education. Benjamin N. Cardozo, of Portuguese-Spanish ancestry, whose forebears came to America before the Revolution, was an associate justice of the Supreme Court of the United States from 1932 to 1938. Two other Jewish Supreme Court justices were Louis D. Brandeis, who served from 1916 to 1939, and Felix Frankfurter, 1939 to 1962. Julius Rosenwald, formerly head of Sears, Roebuck Company, established a fund bearing his name which is "dedicated to the well-being of mankind." Jonas Salk discovered the vaccine to protect people from poliomyelitis. Jewish talent has made significant contributions to other creative arts and sciences. Jews sponsor and support philanthropic activities for orphans, old people, hospitals, sanitariums, and social service agencies. *(The Challenge of Democracy)*

That same text also includes this caption under a picture of Albert Einstein:

> It is ironic that a civilized nation like Germany should try to exterminate the Jews, on the grounds that they were inferior, during the same century in which Albert Einstein and

> Sigmund Freud lived. It would be hard to name two men who had a greater influence on modern thought. *(The Challenge of Democracy)*

Other texts, however, do not heed the warning of the A.C.E. noted above. Consider this example:

> For nearly forty years (1886–1924) the president of the A.F.L. was Samuel Gompers, a cigar-maker. His Dutch-Jewish parents had brought him as a boy from London to New York. Under his shrewd leadership, the A.F. of L. concentrated on what he called "pure and simple" unionism. . . . *(United States History)*

As the A.C.E. said, in illustrating its admonition, "The fact that Samuel Gompers was a Jew has little to do with the rise of the American Federation of Labor."* The practice discouraged here is a common one. World history textbooks have referred to Karl Marx as "of a well-to-do Jewish family" *(The Human Achievement);* to Benjamin Disraeli as belonging "to a converted Jewish family" *(The Record of Mankind)* or as "the brilliant Jewish leader" *(Story of Nations);* and to Leon Trotsky as "a Ukrainian Jew" *(Our Widening World)*. However, other texts offer lengthy biographical portraits of men such as Albert Einstein *(World History and Cultures: The Story of Man's Achievements)* or Haym Salomon *(Rise of the American Nation)* and do not take the opportunity to be *comprehensive* and *concrete* by identifying the Jewish backgrounds of these men.

Not only do textbooks fail to offer adequate de-

---

*A.C.E. Study, p. 105.

scriptions of the diversity that exists and has existed among the American Jewish community (ADL's 1960 report alone quoted references to twenty-nine famous American Jews; today references to only seventeen different American Jews have been found in all the forty-five texts reviewed), they also fail to offer an explanation of the religious beliefs of modern American Jews. Only one civics text and three world histories contain any description whatever of the Jewish religion:

> Differences among denominations result not so much from teaching different ideals as from emphasizing different interpretations of the Scripture. Jewish people accept only the Old Testament as divinely given and look upon Jesus as just a great religious teacher. *(Building Citizenship)*

> Modern Judaism consists of three major groupings: Orthodox Judaism, which emphasizes tradition and observance; Conservative Judaism, which makes adjustments in traditions; and Reform Judaism, which emphasizes the prophetic heritage. All of these groups are essentially agreed upon the ethical and moral teachings of Judaism, the obligation of prayer and worship, and belief in the one God who chose the Hebrews as His own people with a Covenant to reveal Him to mankind. *(Man's Cultural Heritage)*

> Today the word *Jews* refers to those people who believe in the religion of Judaism, the faith started by the ancient Hebrews. Although rituals vary, the Jews today believe in the basic ideas of the ancient Hebrews. These ideas include the following:

1. BELIEF IN ONE GOD . . .
2. BELIEF IN THE TEN COMMANDMENTS . . .
3. BELIEF IN THE IMPORTANCE OF THE TO-
   RAH . . .
4. BELIEF IN THE COMPASSION OF GOD . . .
5. BELIEF IN THE BROTHERHOOD OF ALL
   MANKIND . . .

(*A World History: A Cultural Approach*)

In spite of their outward similarities, each religion is distinctive. Jews take great pride in the belief that they are a chosen people who enjoy God's special favor. Their history, from the appearance of the first tribes in Canaan, contains many examples of God's watchful care for them. The idea that they are a chosen people largely explains why the Jews, unlike Christians and Moslems, do not try to convert others. The Jews feel strongly that their most important mission is to preserve and pass on to their children the precious faith they have inherited from their fathers, in spite of persecution. Their great importance as a people has arisen from their religious ideas. *(Story of Nations)*

For the most part, then, it appears the textbooks reviewed make little effort to build intergroup understanding by the *inclusion* of a *balanced* and *comprehensive* explanation of the diversified heritage and contemporary religious beliefs of the American Jewish people.

F. JEWS AS A RACE

None of the forty-eight books surveyed in 1960 fall into an earlier erroneous practice noticed in the A.C.E.'s 1949 study, that of referring to Jews as a race. Dr. Marcus identified the problem then at hand. "What remains to be done by most of the text-books," he said, "is to make explicit the fact that Jews are not a racial group and beyond that, to explain the nature of races. . . ."* (At that time only two social problems texts explicitly stated that Jews were not a race, and four world histories and one social problems text discussed the question of race.)

The past decade has seen some, albeit insufficient, progress in the direction Dr. Marcus indicated. None of the forty-five books currently reviewed makes the error of referring to the Jews as a race and a greater percentage of them explicitly decry this practice and/or discuss the question of race. Race as a concept is taken up in nine world histories and four social problems texts. (An analysis of their treatment of the topic can be found in Chapter Three.)

Of significance to this section is the action taken by five world histories, one American history, and two social problems texts in explaining why Jews are not a race. What remains still to be done is for more texts to follow the lead of those that make such statements as:

> People are constantly misusing the word *race* when they mean language, religion, culture, or nationality. They speak of the English race, the Jewish race, and the Aryan race, though none of these is a race. . . . The Jews are a mixed people. . . . *(The Challenge of Democracy)*

> In fact, the word *race* is often used incorrectly. Even educated persons sometimes use

---

*ADL Study, p. 22.

race when they mean *religion, nationality* or *language.* For example, there is no Jewish race. *(Our World Through the Ages)*

You may hear people speak of the "Jewish race," or the "French race." These are incorrect uses of the term. The Jews are a group of people who follow the Jewish religion. *(New Dimensions of World History)*

Race is also confused with religion, as is the case of the Jews, or Hebrews. You may have heard people refer to the Jewish race. This is an erroneous use of the word race, because the Jews are simply a group of people who profess Judaism, or the Jewish religion. It is true that the Jews of Biblical times resided in Palestine and belonged either to the Semitic or Armenoid branches of the Mediterranean Caucasoids. In the centuries since then, Judaism has spread widely, and now it is possible to find members of all three large racial groups who profess the Jewish faith. *(A Global History of Man)*

Summary

Compared with the findings of previous reports, the treatment of the Jews in the textbooks examined in 1969 has these characteristics:

A.   World history texts still give considerably more attention to the ancient Hebrews than to later Jewish history. However, a trend toward linking that early tradition to modern times, and toward reminding the student of his and democracy's legacy from Judaism, continues to gain ground, at a high level of quality. There is evidence that social studies texts other than world histories can and should follow this trend.

B. Many textbook accounts of the crucifixion continue to be too superficial to dispel misconceptions concerning the role played by the Jews in that event. Some texts avoid mentioning the crucifixion altogether, while a few still explicitly link the Jews to the death of Jesus in a way likely to increase anti-Semitic feelings on the part of their readers.

C. The infrequent and disjointed references to Jews in medieval and modern European history still deal mainly with persecution and exile. Yet, most texts offer comprehensive discussions of the development of the state of Israel, acknowledging and highlighting the accomplishments of its Jewish people.

D. Jews are mentioned only incidentally by most American history and social problems texts. Although previously negative portrayals of the Jews as a standardized, uniform group are gone from the texts, most of them are not replaced with positive portrayals. There are a very few accounts that do convey a realistic sense of the diversity of the American Jewish population and thus of their similarity to the other peoples of this nation.

E. Textbook passages which make an effort to explain why the Jews should not be referred to as a race are increasing.

The 1949 A.C.E. report warns that:

> . . . overemphasis on persecution—often made in the most humane spirit—leaves many pupils with the impression that the Jews can never be members of a normal, adjusted, accepted group . . . textbooks may intensify an impression that a compulsive destiny dogs the Jews, that their persecution is "normal" and that little can be done to avoid it. *

---

*A.C.E. Study, p. 99.

The implication herein is that as textbooks fail to recognize "Jewish achievements and cooperativeness" in American and world history they contribute to the development of anti-Semitic stereotypes and in fact to the very anti-Semitism that so frequently surfaces in periods of social stress.

We in America are now experiencing such a period, and anti-Semitism does not lie dormant. To the degree that individual textbooks have been found to be ignorant of the A.C.E.'s warning, these books are providing a foundation for forces that attempt to destroy successful intergroup relations.

CHAPTER TWO

TEXTBOOK TREATMENT OF MINORITIES UNDER NAZISM

In early 1960, anti-Semitic desecrations in the United States reached alarming proportions. According to Dr. Marcus, investigators of these acts found that the youth involved "had little knowledge of the human meaning of the Nazi symbols and slogans they had employed."*

The 1960 Anti-Defamation League study concluded that "youth in America appear to be ignorant of the nature and consequences of Hitlerism. In view of the staggering price humanity paid for underestimating this danger in the 1930's, the aims, methods, and consequences of Nazism would seem to be one of history's most important lessons—one not to be neglected in American social studies."†

However, that study found the story of the Nazi holocaust to be flagrantly neglected in social studies textbooks. Only nine of the forty-eight texts reviewed offered a "reasonably clear presentation of systematic persecution and wholesale extermination"; seventeen texts had neglected Nazi genocide altogether; and the remaining twenty-two had "minimized or glossed over important aspects of the topic."

In the latter 1960's anti-Semitic desecrations had

---

*ADL Study, p. 24.
†*Ibid.*

not occurred as frequently as in the beginning of the decade; yet neither are they an event of the past. It is therefore still relevant to examine how textbooks convey that most costly and important lesson of modern history, Nazi persecution and its meaning for all people.

The 1960 report lists five aspects of the subject that the criterion of *inclusion* suggests should be covered by all textbooks. Treatments of these topics were examined in this study as well.

Hitler's "super race" theory: its source in his personality and background, its scientific invalidity, the political uses to which he put it, possible reasons for its effectiveness with his audience, why Jews and other minorities proved useful scapegoats.

Hitler's method of moving against his announced victims in successive stages: from denunciation to incitement to mob action, to economic sanctions, to police brutality, concentration-camp confinement, starvation, torture, gas chamber, and crematorium extermination.

Who the victims were: the predominance of men, women, and children believed to be of Jewish descent but also the inclusion of Catholic and Protestant clergy, of political liberals and other opponents, of non-Jewish Poles, Austrians, and others, as suited Hitler's designs and whims.

The vast numbers of victims: not thousands or hundreds of thousands but millions—including six million Jews.

The reaction of the rest of the world to the developing pattern and to the final revelations: the shock, the Nuremberg war-guilt trials, and the United Nations Genocide Convention.*

---

*ADL Study, p. 24.

As a group, the textbooks examined for this study are hardly more adequate—as measured by the criteria of the study—than those reviewed in 1960. Whereas the past study found one fully satisfactory text and eight that treated certain of the above aspects reasonably well, this report finds four of the forty-five texts to be fully satisfactory and seven that treat one or two of the aspects with reasonable adequacy. The four fully adequate texts are all world histories. Five of those that treat some aspects well are also world histories; one other is an American history text; and the remaining one, a social problems text. Not one other social problems or American history text meets the criteria in covering any of the subtopics. In fact, twelve of the fifteen social problems or civics texts reviewed did not mention the Nazi atrocities at all! In the following pages the omissions and understatements in a majority of the textbooks examined are contrasted with, and underscored by, the adequate accounts that some do offer. Certain of the accounts excerpted are quite long. However, since the purpose of including them is to demonstrate how effectively a textbook can cover each of the topics listed above, they have not been condensed.

ADEQUATE ACCOUNTS

Four world histories are the only textbooks that provide fully satisfactory accounts of the Nazi persecution of minorities. One of these is a later edition of the only text that was found satisfactory in 1960. It contains a five-page section about Hitler's rise to power, his ideology, his methods, and the havoc he created. In discussing Hitler's tactics the text says:

> In *Mein Kampf,* Hitler discussed what has been called *the big lie technique.* He stated in

effect that if a lie is big enough and told often enough, the average person (for whom Hitler had contempt) would believe it. Perhaps his greatest lie was his preaching that the Germans are members of a pure master race called *Aryan*. (The Germans, like most Europeans, are members of the white race, and there is no such thing as a master race or an Aryan race.) Hitler proclaimed that other peoples were inferior, fit only to serve the Germans. . . . Hitler knew that when hate enters the heart, reason often leaves the mind, and that an unreasoning people are easily led. That is one reason why he fanned the flames of anti-Semitism. He often lied to German nationalists by telling them that Germany had not really lost World War I, but had been sold out by Jews and radicals on the home front. He asserted that German Jews did not belong in Germany because they were not pure Germans. In the same breath he would denounce Jews as communists and capitalists. As dictator, Hitler was to make wider use of the scapegoat technique against Jews than any other ruler in history. . . .

Terror a tool of the Nazi dictatorship. In Nazi Germany, aged Jews were compelled to scrub streets on their hands and knees while Brown Shirts stood over them with clubs. Jewish-owned shops were boycotted or wrecked. Ultimately most Jews lost all their property. Synagogues were burned to the ground. Jews and Christians with some Jewish blood were barred from the professions and fired from their jobs. Jews lost their citizenship. Many of the world's most famous writers, musicians, and scientists, including Albert Einstein, sought refuge in other lands. By the end of World War II, six million Jews had lost their lives in Nazi-held lands. Many of these were sent to concentration camps. There they were deliberately starved, infected with disease, placed in deadly gas chambers, or burned to death in specially constructed ovens. Some were used as guinea pigs in medical experiments which were more savage than scientific. . . .

Terror was also the tool which was used to get rid of liberals, socialists, Communists, and even Nazis who were suspected of challenging the Führer's authority. (*Our World Through the Ages*)

As the earlier study said of this account, "the wording 'some Jewish blood' with its connotation of a racial rather than a religious or ethnic group may be unfortunate; however the remainder of this passage has the virtue of presenting German Jews as real and gifted people and of being explicit as to how they were murdered."* Perhaps a more adequate explanation of whom Hitler considered to be Jews is in the following *comprehensive* account from a text that devotes more than seven pages to covering the aspects of Nazism listed earlier.

Hitler blamed the Jews for most of Germany's ills. Pacifism, revolutionary communism, the Versailles Treaty—these were part of a Jewish plot to wreck Germany and gain control of the world, he said. Among the 60 million inhabitants of Germany were less than 600,000 Jews (not counting Germans who were part

---

*ADL Study, p. 26.

Jewish). Less than 1 per cent of the population, this minority group included many members of the professions and the arts, some of whom had made noteworthy gifts to their country's culture.

In April of 1933 these people were attacked by government decrees that increased in severity as time went on. They were forbidden to hold office; their businesses and professions were boycotted. On May 10, 1933, all books by Jewish authors were ordered burned. Orchestras were forbidden to play the music of Mendelssohn and other Jewish composers. In 1935 the so-called Nuremberg Laws defined a Jew as any person with one Jewish grandparent and deprived all such persons of citizenship. Jews were forbidden to marry non-Jews. They might not teach in any educational institution, write or publish, sell books or antiques, act on stage or screen, exhibit paintings or give concerts, work in a bank or hospital, or belong to labor unions. They could not collect unemployment insurance and were not eligible for charity.

The persecution of the Jews moved to nationwide violence in 1938. One November day a Jewish teen-ager, made desperate by the Nazi treatment of his parents, shot one of the secretaries from the German embassy in Paris. After the news reached Germany, organized mobs looted Jewish stores and shops throughout Germany. They forced their way into Jewish homes, beat the occupants, robbed the houses. They burned and dynamited synagogues. Then, the state ordered the Jews—

not the offenders—to pay a huge fine and restore the damaged properties.

Toward the end of World War II, as the Allied troops pushed into Germany, the greatest of Nazi crimes were uncovered. In the vast concentration camps to which Jews were herded like cattle during the war, they found the gas ovens in which millions of lives had been taken, the bodies of slave laborers who had evidently starved to death, and living dead who had been tortured or used as the victims of medical experiments. When the final count was made after the war, it was clear that between 1939 and 1945 the number of Jews in Nazi-controlled Europe had slipped from 9,739,200 to 3,505,800. Thus a horrified world accused the followers of Adolf Hitler with murdering more than six million Jews. It is said that another six million persons in Poland, Czechoslovakia, Russia, and so forth, were also victims of the Nazis. (*World History and Cultures: The Story of Man's Achievements*)

The grim story told above is further intensified by the inclusion of a picture of "emaciated prisoners of war, who had forgotten to smile, beginning to learn once again" (*World History and Cultures: The Story of Man's Achievements*). Neither this text nor the others with satisfactory accounts fail to remind the reader that Nazism was a symbol of oppression and persecution for Christians as well as Jews. Following are examples of those timely reminders:

The Nazis persecuted Protestants and Catholics as well as Jews. The Protestant Pastor Martin Niemöller was arrested and sent to a concentration camp for opposing Hitler.

Priests found it difficult and, at times, impossible to hold church services or to perform the rites of the Catholic Church. Many of them were arrested for what Hitler called meddling in political affairs. Increasingly, Christianity itself came under attack since it taught kindness and mercy, humility and self-sacrifice, virtues scorned by the Nazis. (*The Pageant of World History*)

Inasmuch as the Nazis put the State above everything else, they wanted to control religion as well as education. Hitler insisted that all Protestants join in a single church. This they were willing to do; but they were not willing to accept the bishop he chose or to teach Christianity according to Nazi ideas. (Many Nazis wished the Christians to repudiate the Old Testament.) Hitler had his way, but many pastors resisted and some of them were sent to concentration camps.

Hitler signed an agreement with the Roman Catholic Church promising not to interfere with its schools, but he later violated this agreement. The Nazis tried to influence parents to take their children out of Catholic schools. Furthermore, they did their best to suppress the Catholic youth movement. They wanted the young people to belong entirely to the Nazi state and to be subjected to no other influences. In spite of the persecution they received, the Catholics did not give in on matters of doctrine, though many of them supported the Nazi state. (*World History and Cultures: The Story of Man's Achievements*)

The most *concrete* and *comprehensive* account of world revulsion and the Nuremberg war crime trials is this one excerpted from a world history that devotes more than five pages to Hitler's actions against the Jews.

The military occupation of Germany revealed to the world the full extent of the horrors of German concentration camps. As you have read, the Nazi policy of extermination led to the death of millions of people. More than 6 million of the estimated 10 million Jews living in Europe had been killed by the Nazis. Many had died of disease and starvation in concentration camps; many others had been shot, hanged, or suffocated in gas chambers. Some were subjected to horrible tortures, serving as subjects for so-called "scientific" experimentation on the human body. The Nazi victims also included almost 6 million non-Jewish Europeans—Poles, Czechs, Russians, Dutch, French, and gypsies.

Beginning in November 1945 and continuing for almost a year, a special international court met at Nuremberg, Germany, to try major Nazi leaders who had taken part in these murders, and had been captured. Hitler was dead, and some of his highest officers had escaped to Spain and Latin America. But many of the top leaders had been captured. The court tried twenty-two of the principal Nazi leaders for "conspiracy to wage aggressive war," "crimes against the peace," and "crimes against humanity" in the extermination camps, the slave-labor camps, and in the conquered countries. Twelve were sentenced to death, seven to life imprisonment, and three were acquitted. The court also declared the Nazi Party a criminal organization.

The Nuremberg trials were unprecedented. For thousands of years the conduct of warfare had been governed by rules, customs, and conventions (certain kinds of international agreements). However, this was the first time that leaders of a country were brought to trial for starting a war. The trials were widely criticized on the grounds that there was no legal precedent for punishing the leaders of a defeated nation. Some people argued that in trying only Germans and not possible war criminals of other nations, the court was violating accepted ideas of justice. Others felt that the trials were an act of vengeance on the part of the victorious powers.

Defenders of the trials argued that, although the court was specially created, the laws by which it acted did exist, uncodified, in various Hague conventions, League of Nations agreements, and international treaties. In addition, it was thought that the trials would help preserve peace and forward the development of international law. They did in fact lead to the United Nations adoption in 1948 of a convention against *genocide*—the systematic extermination of an entire people or national group.

Trials of other war criminals continued for many years in postwar Germany. Hundreds of ex-Nazis were prosecuted—not only high-ranking officers but also camp guards, minor officials, and doctors who had taken part in medical "experiments." (*Men and Nations*)

Each of the four world histories from which the above accounts are taken covers all five subjects: racist theory, increasing brutality, diversity of victims, numbers killed, and world reaction. Seven other texts cover only one or two of these topics in a manner judged adequate by the criteria. Only one account in a social problems text is judged adequate —not so much for its coverage of Nazi persecutions as for the skillful way it warns against the consequences of intergroup conflict and prejudice.

> Prejudice forms the psychological basis for intergroup conflicts, and once these conflicts are begun they can become violent. Most of us have experienced prejudice only in its milder forms and do not know how dangerous it can become. The inhumane things that can be done by civilized people are incredible. When group feeling becomes crystallized under irresponsible leadership, persecution is often the result.
>
> The almost inconceivably barbarous Nazi persecution of the Jews and other people which took place in the twentieth century was done by one of the most civilized nations in the world. Under the leadership of a fanatical and ruthless leader, the Germans were conditioned to accept and participate in persecutions that included slave labor, torture, starvation, mass murder, medical atrocities on human guinea pigs, and concentration camps equipped with gas chambers and ovens for burning human corpses. It is estimated that more than six million of the Jews throughout Europe were exterminated by the Nazis within a decade.
>
> A study of mob actions and riots against

minorities which have occurred in America and in many other countries is also sobering. It shows that Germans are not unique in their capacity to become inhumanly cruel and violent when seized by prejudice and stirred up by fanatics. (*The Challenge of Democracy*)

The single American history text that satisfies the criteria for coverage of some of the topics concludes its relevant passages with the following account of the Nuremberg trials:

For the victorious Allies, however, there still remained the question of what to do with the Nazi leaders who had surrounded Hitler and helped him plan and carry out his war of aggression.

The victorious nations studied records left by Hitler and his followers. These records described in detail how the Nazis had planned to turn Europe into a German empire. In the concentration camps, grim evidence was found of the Nazi campaign to destroy the Jewish people of Europe. A shocked world learned that six million Jews had been murdered in these camps.

Great Britain, France, the Soviet Union, and the United States set up a special court of judges from many nations. In this court, the chief Nazi political and military leaders were tried. They were accused of plotting aggression against their neighbor nations. They were also charged with crimes against humanity, such as the heartless mass executions committed in the concentration camps.

Day after day the huge collection of evidence was revealed in the courtroom at Nuremberg (NYOO-rem-burg), Germany. Each defendant was given a fair chance to answer the charges. The trial lasted for months. Finally the court condemned some of the guilty prisoners to die. Others received prison terms. (*Story of the American Nation*)

In this section selections from six textbooks have been excerpted to demonstrate how well these texts convey to their readers the grim truth of what happened under the symbol and slogans of Nazism. Five other texts—world histories—are also reasonably adequate in conveying that message to their young readers. However, taken together these texts represent less than 25 per cent of the forty-five textbooks examined for this study. The inadequacy of the remaining texts is reviewed in the following section.

INADEQUATE ACCOUNTS

Social problems texts. Of the fifteen social problems texts examined, the brief treatment found in the one quoted in the previous section is the best. What of the other texts? Twelve ignore the topic completely. Even those that include a passing reference to Hitler say nothing about Nazi persecutions, scapegoating, or genocide. One of them manages to devote five pages to Hitler without mentioning the atrocities he caused to be committed. Two others refer to Nazi persecutions, apparently on the assumption that the reader is so familiar with the subject matter that further details are not necessary. In comparing due process with dictatorial techniques, one of the two simply states:

For example, Hitler's dictatorship in Germany "disposed of" millions of Jews without providing legal procedures. (*Government in Our Republic*)

Another text captions a well-known dramatic photograph of refugees behind the fence of a concentration camp as follows:

> At the end of World War II, the inmates of a German concentration camp, their faces reflecting despair and fear, await liberation after months of captivity. The Nazis forced thousands of people into such camps, without trial or even formal accusations of crime. (*Communities and Government in a Changing World*)

This statement fails to meet even the most obvious of our criteria, *validity*. The term "thousands" is so great an understatement it can hardly be considered accurate. In addition, the phrase "without even formal accusations of crime" implies to the uninformed that those interred had indeed committed criminal acts.

American histories. In contrast to the social problems texts, most American histories do deal somewhat with Nazi persecutions. Only one text leaves out any mention whatever of the atrocities. However, three others offer merely a sentence or two. The remaining ten texts, while containing passages about various aspects of the topic, cannot, by the criteria, be considered adequate; in some cases they are actually misleading. The better of these passages fail to provide enough detail to meet the criteria of *realism* and *concreteness*. They fail to communicate to the student the true horror of the day in tangible, real terms.

> *The "death factories."* As the armies swarmed over Germany, the extent of the Nazis' bar-

barity was brought to light—Allied soldiers came upon the infamous German concentration camps. These "death factories" housed not only political "enemies" of Hitler and his Nazi party but also many Jews—the unfortunate people whom the Nazis had especially singled out for horrible persecution. The invading forces found that over *six million* Jews had been murdered in these concentration camps in accordance with a diabolically planned system for dealing death.

A new word was coined to name this incredible slaughter of whole peoples: genocide. Eisenhower personally inspected one of these murder camps so that he could always bear witness that the accounts of Nazi brutality were not mere Allied propaganda. Amid pitiable scenes, survivors in these camps welcomed as soldiers of humanity itself the troops who liberated them. (*The Adventure of the American People*)

The shocking revelation of Nazi horrors. The first outbursts of joy and relief at the end of the war in Europe were soon dulled by the shocking news that came out of Germany. As the Allied armies occupied the conquered country, the full extent of Nazi horrors came to light. For the first time, the whole world heard of bloodcurdling crimes the Nazis had perpetrated in their awful concentration camps. In one of the most terrible displays of brutality ever to be seen in human history, the Nazis had created these camps, or "death factories," to destroy their "political enemies"

and to exterminate the entire Jewish population.

With a horror almost beyond belief, the
world learned that 6,000,000 men, women,
and children, most of them Jews, had been
slaughtered after suffering unspeakable anxieties, agonies, indignities, and tortures. General
Eisenhower visited one of the camps so that
he could testify that reports of Nazi atrocities
were not Allied propaganda. (*Rise of the
American Nation*)

The first of these two passages does little more
than reinforce other textbook images of the Jews as
an anachronistic, "unfortunate" people. The passage
seems to focus more on the Allied "soldiers of humanity" than Hitler's evil. The second passage is
hardly explicit or *concrete* with its use of such emo-
tive terms as "bloodcurdling," "agonies," and "unspeakable anxieties." Moreover, six million is hardly
considered by most authorities a *valid* estimate of the
total number—irrespective of ethnic background—of
men, women, and children slaughtered by the Nazis.
This textbook further dilutes the horror of the Nazi
persecutions in a picture caption which gives as
much attention to the quality of the photo as it does
to its subject:

In one of the most striking pictures of World
War II, the famous photographer Margaret
Bourke-White photographed these bewildered
prisoners in the notorious Buchenwald concentration camp as horrified American troops arrived to set them free. (*Rise of the American
Nation*)

Three other texts offer accounts of the Nazi
persecution with implications that are neither *con-*

crete nor *valid*. The following passages imply that the reason the Jews were persecuted was that they opposed the Nazi state:

> The Allied soldiers found prison camps—called concentration camps—where starving Jewish men, women, and children had been penned up. The Nazis had also operated gas chambers where Jews and other Nazi opponents had been heartlessly put to death. (*The Free and the Brave*)

> In his march to power, Adolf Hitler ruthlessly destroyed all who stood in his way. He told the German people that it was the Jews who had betrayed Germany. He had a particular dislike for people of the Jewish faith, and under his direction millions of Jews were imprisoned, tortured, and killed. Jewish property and businesses were taken over by the government. (*History of Our United States*)

> Though anyone who spoke out against the government was punished, German Jews suffered most at the hands of the Nazis. Hitler and his top advisers declared their intention of establishing a "master race" in Germany. Since the Jews did not fit into Hitler's idea of a "pure" German race, they were ruthlessly persecuted. (*A History of the United States*).

One text that was criticized in the 1960 report retains its offensive account.

> Under Hitler the Germans once more became a proud people with high hopes for the future. But this gain was achieved at heavy cost. People were no longer free in Germany; those who disagreed with Hitler dared not say so. Many

lived in dread of the Nazi secret police. The Nazis imprisoned, tortured, killed, or drove from the country anyone who dared speak out against them. They were especially cruel to Jews, whom they blamed for all of Germany's troubles. Jews were stripped of their property, and thousands of them were sent to concentration camps, where they suffered starvation, torture, and death. Some six million European Jews had been destroyed by the Nazis by the close of World War II. (*This Is America's Story*)

This passage too implies that the Nazi persecution of Jews was in response to Jewish actions rather than as a result of irrational beliefs and policies of their Führer. In addition, the juxtaposition of a brief and sterile reference to the holocaust with a reference to the Germans as a "once more proud people" is particularly insensitive. One other American history text also engages in this practice. In the following passage, what happened to the Jews is presented so blandly that it is made to seem almost inconsequential as compared with Germany's renewed growth.

Individuals are unimportant in the Nazi state. Under the dictatorship of Hitler and the Nazis, Germany was transformed into a united, energetic nation. Once more the German people took great pride in their country. Industry boomed and large public works were undertaken. But these gains were won at the cost of human liberties. Every phase of life in Germany was controlled by the Nazi Party. Every individual had to bow to the will of the state, which encouraged the ruthless use of force to establish the supremacy of the "master race." Freedom of speech disappeared, newspapers were muzzled, schools became centers of Nazi propaganda, and freedom of religion was restricted. Labor and industry alike were placed under the close regulation of the state. Giving as their goal the establishment of a Greater Germany for the "master race," the Nazis began repressive policies which eventually led to imprisonment, forced labor, and death for millions of Jews. (*The Making of Modern America*)

A final example comes from a book which presents an account of the Nuremberg war trials both in its text and as a separate highlight; yet it never presents the actions that had precipitated the need for the trials.

The International Military Tribunal, composed of the victorious allies, was to sit in judgment on the twenty-two highest officials of Nazi Germany. They were charged with responsibility for the war and crimes against humanity. Among these were mass murder, enslavement, looting, and atrocities against civilians. It was hoped that the trials would be a step forward in strengthening international law. Many saw the trials as a means of preserving peace and civilization, though others criticized them as acts of vengeance.

On October 1, 1946, came the fateful verdicts. Eleven Nazi leaders were sentenced to death by hanging for crimes against humanity. Others were given prison sentences ranging from ten years to life. Several were found not guilty. The principle of individual responsibility for war crimes, irrespective of official position, was thus established. (*Our American Republic*)

The above passages individually touch on one or more of the five subtopics. Yet they do so in a way that violates one or more of the criteria of *validity, realism, unity, balance,* and *comprehensiveness.*

World histories. The books in this category perform considerably better than do those in the area of American history or social problems. Four are judged fully satisfactory and have been quoted earlier in this chapter. In addition five others review some of the subtopics with reasonable adequacy. However, six world histories are too incomplete to be of any use in conveying to students the realities of Nazism. The briefest of these accounts is this sentence from a discussion of the "cost of the war":

> Many millions of civilians lost their lives, including six million Jews alone, who were murdered on Hitler's order. (*A Global History of Man*)

Another text does not even indicate that Hitler had pursued a systematic policy of Jewish extermination. Instead it focuses on the "problems" of the Allies in punishing the Nazis for previously undetailed crimes.

> The war left many political problems to be worked out. During the war the Allies had warned the Nazis repeatedly that their leaders would be held responsible for plunging the world into war and for pursuing such beastly policies. More than a score of the German leaders were brought to trial before an international military tribunal in Nuremberg, Ger-

many. Here the awful stories of torture and mass murders were recounted. Eleven of the men were sentenced as "war criminals" to die by hanging, three were acquitted, and the rest were given long prison sentences. The new local governments in Germany meted out punishment to many more. (*A History of the World*)

One world history text had only this to offer concerning Hitler's racist theories and the Jews.

Hitler and his close associates made campaigns and speeches from one end of the country to the other. They used the radio skillfully and made their meetings dramatic emotional experiences for their followers. Hitler boasted, inflamed, won followers by preaching hatred against different groups, depending on his audience—sometimes capitalists, sometimes Communists. Above all, he preached hatred against the Jews. He developed an elaborate cult of German "racial superiority," encouraging Germans to believe in themselves as the "master race," destined to rule the world and be served by all other "races." *(Our Widening World)*

Beyond its lack of *comprehensiveness* the most obvious inadequacy of this account is its failure to show the irrationality of Hitler's beliefs and their results. Merely to report historical facts as they occur is not to educate. While this study does not expect editorialization, it does demand that students be told all that is factually correct and relevant to a topic. Some facts require explanation if the student is not to be misled. Simply putting quotes around the word *race* does not explain the falseness and lack of scientific validity in Hitler's or any similar theories of a master or superior race. A better approach is taken by another text that is nevertheless considered inadequate for failing to meet the criterion of *comprehensiveness;* it is not explicit enough about who the other Nazi victims were and what was done to them and the Jews.

> *Hitler based the Nazi claim to supremacy on the idea that Germans were a superior race.* In one important respect Hitler's National Socialism differed from Mussolini's Fascism. Hitler made the absurd claim that the Germans were not merely a *nation,* like France or England or Italy, but a *race.* All Germany's troubles, he said, stemmed from the fact that "pure" German blood had been mixed with other strains such as that of the Jews. So he took away German citizenship from all persons of Jewish descent. They could no longer vote, hold office, edit newspapers, or hold positions in business and the professions. They could not even marry "pure" Germans. Many Jews fled the country. Those who remained were subject to ill treatment and persecution. Then during World War II Hitler's government decided to do away with them. Millions of Jews, along with other prisoners, were sent to concentration camps and systematically and brutally murdered.
>
> There was, of course, no basis for Hitler's notions of race. Scientific studies indicate that there is no such thing as a pure race, to say nothing of a superior race. Both the Germans and the Jews are of mixed ancestry. But Hitler and his party leaders found the Jews a con-

venient scapegoat on whom to lay the blame
when anything went wrong. (*The History of
Our World*)

It is perhaps interesting to note that the last
three texts quoted above were examined and criticized in the 1960 study as well. The two other
texts that were judged inadequate offer only the following:

Hitler soon made Germany over into a cen-
tralized, totalitarian state ruled by him and his
Nazi party. The Nazis controlled every facet
of German life. Concentration camps—places
for the confinement of prisoners of war, persons with feared political beliefs, and refugees
—were built and packed with people Hitler
and his Nazis did not like. These included
Communists, Socialists, the liberal minded,
and the Jews. Under some of the more fanatic
Nazis, these camps were turned into scenes of
horror where gas ovens extinguished the lives
of millions of Jews. The Jews were singled out
for the special hatred of the Nazi. (*Man's Cultural Heritage*)

The Nazis believed that they belonged to a
so-called "pure Aryan race," that "Aryan
blood" was superior to that of all other people, and that they were destined to rule the
world. These Nazi ideas were completely un-
scientific.

The Nazis were anti-Semitic—that is, they
were bitterly opposed to the Jews. They believed that people of the Jewish religion or
those descended from Jews should be denied
all rights, driven from Germany, or exe-
cuted. . . .

Under the Nazis, religious groups were ridiculed, persecuted, and attacked. Jews were hounded, deprived of rights, branded with the Star of David, and sent to torture and death in concentration camps. (*A World History: A Cultural Approach*)

Neither of these accounts is specific enough in discussing what was done to the Jews to be considered *comprehensive*. In addition the former may inadvertently reinforce anti-Semitic stereotypes in the reader's mind by linking Jews to "Communists, Socialists and the liberal minded." As the 1949 A.C.E. study said, "Equally disturbing is the combining of Jews with other groups which lack prestige with many Americans. The effectiveness of the transfer mechanism is well known; the possible psychological repercussions of such passages . . . should be more carefully guarded against by textbook writers."*

SUMMARY

For purposes of comparison with the 1960 report a summary of the material in this section can best be presented primarily in quantitative terms.

Overview

1960
Nine out of forty-eight textbooks analyzed gave reasonably adequate presentations of Nazi persecution of minority groups. Only one of these fully met the established criteria. Twenty-two books slighted, mini-

---

*A.C.E. Study p. 103.

mized, or glossed over important aspects of the topic. Seventeen omitted it entirely.
1969
Eleven out of forty-five textbooks examined give reasonably adequate presentations of Nazi persecution of minority groups. Only four fully meet the established criteria. Twenty-one books slight, minimize, or gloss over important aspects of the topic. Thirteen texts omit it entirely.

Or, looking at it another way:

	1960 study (48 books)	1969 study (45 books)
Texts giving fully adequate coverage	2.1%	8.8%
Texts giving reasonably adequate coverage	18.8%	24.4%
Texts slighting or minimizing the topic	45.9%	46.7%
Texts omitting the topic entirely	35.4%	28.9%

When the texts are classified by subject-matter areas, the results are as follows:

SOCIAL PROBLEMS OR CIVICS TEXTS
1960
Eleven out of sixteen books omitted the topic; four treated it inadequately. One gave it reasonably adequate treatment.
1969
Twelve out of fifteen books omit the topic; two treat it inadequately. One gives it reasonably adequate treatment.

AMERICAN HISTORY TEXTS
1960
Five out of sixteen books omitted the topic; nine treated it inadequately. Two gave it reasonably adequate treatment.
1969
One of the fifteen books omits the topic; thirteen treat it inadequately. One gives it reasonably adequate treatment.

WORLD HISTORY
1960
Of sixteen world histories, fifteen covered the modern period. None omitted the topic, but nine treated it inadequately. Five offered reasonably adequate treatments. In one text the treatment was fully satisfactory.
1969
None of the fifteen world histories omit the topic. Six treat it inadequately. Five offer reasonably adequate treatment. In four the treatment is fully satisfactory.

The 1960 study concludes that:

> . . . the great majority of textbooks do not serve the function that might be reasonably expected of them in this area: to present students with a basic overview of the topic of Nazi victimization and slaughter of vast numbers of innocent people. Much needs to be done by textbook authors and publishers to assure that American youth will know the implications of the swastika. . . .*

Yet nearly a decade later we find that "much" has not been done. Many textbooks still fail to fulfill their responsibility to American youth. And their failure may be tragic indeed, for those who withhold the lessons of history may be dooming other generations to repeat its mistakes.

---

*ADL Study, p. 37.

CHAPTER THREE

TEXTBOOK TREATMENT OF BLACK AMERICANS

In 1949 the American Council on Education, in their study of teaching materials, concluded that:

A. The black American's position in contemporary society was ignored by the average textbook.

B. Most references to blacks were to the period before 1876, picturing them as slaves and bewildered freed men and thus perpetuating the stereotype of a childlike, inferior group of people.

C. There was a great lack of scientific data on man and the question of race.

D. Even more inadequate than the written material in these textbooks were the illustrations showing blacks in American life.

In 1960 those same criticisms, as applied to the textbooks then examined, continued to be valid. Yet the decade of the 1960's has seen a new awareness of black people and their problems. They are demanding recognition in our contemporary society, and they are being recognized. Is this recognition reflected in the social studies textbooks that serve American schoolchildren?

A. Position of blacks in contemporary society

In 1960 it was said that "very little progress has been made since the late 1940's in this area. In fact, the cardinal weakness in present texts is a striking lack of any serious discussions of the American Negro's current struggles and changing status."* At that time, of the twenty-four texts (eight in each subject area) analyzed, thirteen omitted all reference to blacks in contemporary society.† Today, of the forty-five books examined only ten omit all reference to black Americans in contemporary society, and nine of these are world histories. As a committee of eminent historians from the history department of the University of California at Berkeley said, "This civil rights revolution seems to us to be one of the major historical events of the mid-twentieth century and to demand full treatment in any American History textbook."‡ Further, these men go on to explain what they mean by full treatment: "The gains that have been made should be described realistically and not as an ode to the inevitable justice and progress of the democratic system. It should be made clear that the outcome of the civil rights struggle is still in doubt, and that the inequalities are so great as to defy quick remedy by even the most vigorous effort."**

All American histories reviewed in the current study as well as all social problems and civics texts —with the exception of one remarkably unaware book—meet the criterion of *inclusion* by offering some information on the contemporary black man.

---

*ADL Study, p. 38.

†Although the 1960 ADL Study selected forty-eight texts for review, on some topics only one-half of that number were analyzed.

‡Kenneth M. Stampp, Winthrop D. Jordan, Lawrence W. Levine, Robert L. Middlekaufe, Charles G. Sellers, and George W. Stockings, Jr., "The Negro in American History Textbooks," *Integrated Education,* October–November 1964, p. 13.

**Ibid.

Most of them, however, could be judged inadequate on the basis of the lack of frankness—as necessitated by the criteria of *balance, comprehensiveness, and realism*—in their treatment of the need and reasons for the current civil rights movement. In the textbook coverage of the contemporary black American, quality ranks far below quantity. Only five books (four American histories and one social problems text) offer what might be considered exceptional or satisfactory treatments. Nine other texts (three American histories, five social problems texts, and one world history) cover the subject well or with reasonable adequacy. In twenty texts the accounts are so brief, perfunctory, or noncommittal that they can only be considered inadequate. Ten others, as has been mentioned before, do not cover the topic.

Therefore less than one-third of the textbooks selected for their popularity in American classrooms offer reasonably good accounts of the black man in contemporary society. Since it is impossible in these few pages to excerpt more than a small number of the many passages related to this topic, accounts relevant to four different subtopics will be contrasted to give the reader an idea of the type and range of textual treatments available.

Civil rights. Too few texts offer overall discussions of the civil rights movement or convey what it means to be a black in contemporary society; those that do contain contrasting treatments. One social problems text discusses the blacks' desire to secure equality. This same text next offers the arguments of those who oppose integration. Finally it concludes that "Democracy offers Negroes opportunities" and points out reasons why this is true. Pertinent selections from that text follow:

The Negro seeks greater equality. One of our largest minority groups in the United States is the Negro. Removed from bondage less than one hundred years ago, the Negro continues to work for many of the rights and privileges that other American citizens enjoy. Negroes seek to be treated as individuals, rather than as members of a minority group. As members of a minority group they feel like second-class citizens.

First, they seek greater equality of opportunity. . . .

Second, the Negro strives for greater legal and political equality. . . .

Finally, he wants all forms of segregation abolished. . . .

Many Americans agree that Negroes are entitled to greater economic opportunity, to greater legal and political equality, and to an end to segregation. . . . But though a probable majority think the Negro is entitled to all of these reforms, including an end to segregation, this country is not unanimous on this point. Many white people in the North as well as the South desire to continue racial segregation. . . .

Arguments of those who oppose integration. A leading spokesman for one Southern viewpoint is Thomas R. Waring, editor of the Charleston (S.C.) *News and Courier.* In *Harper's Magazine* for January, 1956, he contends that health standards, cultural standards, and intellectual development among Negroes are lower than among whites, and that crime rates are higher. Southern whites, he says, do not want their children exposed to these lower standards nor to dangers of violence, and are particularly worried that lowered racial barriers will encourage interracial marriage. . . .

Democracy offers Negroes opportunities. Any major social change evolves slowly in a democracy. Although many people fret at this slowness, in fact much has been accomplished in the last century toward granting equality to Negroes. Desegregation laws and civil rights commissions do not provide neat and quick solutions, but they do provide a framework wherein our democracy can move slowly and surely in the direction of equality. Negroes are slowly gaining a greater position of dignity and respect in American life. (*The Challenge of Democracy*)

While the authors of this text state no direct untruths and do not editorialize, the point of view of the passage is so neutral as to suggest a lack of *balance*. This account, at its best, does little more than defend slowness in granting equal rights; at its worst it may reinforce racial stereotypes. By contrast consider the following passages, which are a small portion of one social problems text's thirty-five-page chapter "Curbing Prejudice and Discrimination."

What the Negro wants. The Negro American today has much the same goals and aspirations as the average white citizen. He wants equality of opportunity for himself and his family. This means, among other things, the right to earn his living at a job appropriate to his abilities and interests. He resents being held down to menial low-paying jobs because of his race. He wants to be able to better his place in society.

For his children the Negro wants to be able to provide a good education, so they can make something of themselves. . . .

The Negro American wants equality before the law. . . .

The Negro American today wants the right to full and free participation in city, county, state, and Federal elections. . . . He wants good housing for his family. . . . He wants the same privilege other citizens have of securing food and lodging away from home at the same rates charged to all.

Finally, the Negro American today desires respect—not merely tolerance. He wants more than an end to segregation. He aspires to the dignity and fair treatment that all Americans desire for themselves. He wants to belong, to be able to participate fully and freely in the life of his community. . . .

Racial discrimination is based on false premises. There are a good many misconceptions and false notions about the races of mankind. Perhaps you are familiar with some of them. Some people believe, for example, that the white race is superior to all other races. Responsible and competent scientists challenge this idea. . . . The great bulk of research seems to support the belief that the range of mental capacities in all races is much the same.

. . . The noted American anthropologist, Franz Boas, stated: "If we were to select the most intelligent, imaginative, energetic, and emotionally stable third of mankind, all races would be represented." The implications of this scientifically established truth are obvious—if we can provide equal educational opportunities and environmental advantages for all our citizens, the so-called "inferiority" of certain minority groups will tend to disappear. *(Problems of Democracy)*

Two junior high school American histories use the following quite different approaches in introducing the civil rights movement to their readers:

Civil Rights. Your rights as a citizen are called your *civil rights.* Most of our people have always felt that all Americans should be treated fairly and equally and have an equal chance to improve their lives. Nonetheless, we have other groups of people who have not wanted to see equal rights for all.

We have many minority groups in America. Slowly, but surely, minority groups have gained more rights, but certain religious groups, Indians, Japanese-Americans, Negroes, and Puerto Ricans still feel that they are denied many rights. *(History of Our United States)*

Unfinished Business: Civil Rights. From the 1950's on, no issue drew more deserved attention than the situation of the American Negro. Despite the Thirteenth, Fourteenth, and Fifteenth amendments to the Constitution, the Negro had been discriminated against by law and by custom in all parts of the country. He was, in short, a "second-class citizen" denied his civil rights. The attempts of organized Negroes and whites to arouse new concern over this blot on American democracy

> is known as the civil rights movement. (*The Free and the Brave*)

The first of the two passages just quoted notes that many blacks "still feel that they are denied many rights." Contrast that approach with the definitive statements of the second passage. In the former the student is left to form his own judgment as to whether the "feelings" of minorities are valid. In the latter he is told what is the reality of the situation. Offered as an example of the weakness of the first text, the following passage represents all that it has to say concerning civil rights under President Lyndon B. Johnson's 1964–1968 term in office.

> *Domestic Affairs.* The major domestic problems which confronted President Johnson were civil rights, violence in the cities, and the reaction to his Vietnamese policy. Negroes became increasingly active in seeking political and social equality. Although civil rights acts were passed in 1964 and 1965, many Negroes did not think that the government was moving quickly enough to end segregation. The assassination of the Negro civil rights leader Dr. Martin Luther King, Jr., in April, 1968, led to major outbreaks of violence. (*History of Our United States*)

Three world histories also comment on the civil rights movement in this country. The introduction to the strongest and longest of these accounts is quoted below:

> American Negroes had been freed from slavery during the Civil War. In order to guarantee their *civil rights*—that is, their equality as American citizens—three constitutional

amendments were adopted soon afterward. Negroes, however, did not actually attain equal rights, but were discriminated against as "second-class citizens." In many regions of the United States, both north and south, laws and customs prohibited them from voting and from obtaining decent education, jobs, and housing. Segregation—separation from whites, particularly in schools and housing—kept Negroes out of the mainstream of American life. (*Men and Nations*)

However, despite the encouraging introduction, this text contains only four other paragraphs on the civil rights movement. In a triumph of brevity it summarizes some of the most important and dramatic years in contemporary American history:

The civil rights drive aroused determined resistance, both by legal means and by violence. However, in the eleven years that followed *Brown v. Topeka,* the federal government enacted four civil rights laws to end discrimination in voting, education, employment, and public facilities. In the late 1960's some Negro groups, believing that Negro legal rights were now well safeguarded, began advocating more militant action to gain social equality. (*Men and Nations*)

The Supreme Court and school desegregation. This topic is included in virtually all the texts that treat the blacks in contemporary society. However, the quality of the accounts differs sharply. While the majority merely report the Supreme Court's decision of 1954 and leave the reader to assume that henceforward schools will be desegregated, a good number do relate the difficulties in enforcing the

court order. A very few others discuss school segregation in the North. Examples that reflect this as-
sessment follow. The first are from American histories.

> The Court recognized that, in some communi-
> ties, long-established customs would make a
> quick change difficult. The Chief Justice an-
> nounced that the Court would hold special
> hearings to consider proposals by the states
> for changing public school systems.
>
> Changing from segregated to integrated
> schools presented different problems. In some
> communities, like Louisville, Kentucky, and
> Baltimore, Maryland, the schools were inte-
> grated rather quickly. In others, the process
> has moved slowly, and in a few instances trou-
> ble has arisen. (*Story of the American Na-
> tion*)
>
> *The Supreme Court rules on the schools.* An
> important event of President Eisenhower's first
> administration was neither an action of his
> nor of the Congress but a decision of the Su-
> preme Court. On May 17, 1954, the Court
> declared unanimously that state laws requiring
> Negro children to attend separate public
> schools were unconstitutional. In a later deci-
> sion the Supreme Court directed that
> "a prompt and reasonable start" should be
> made toward allowing both white and Negro
> pupils to attend the same schools. In some
> states much was done to carry out the Court's
> decision. Other states proceeded slowly, while
> in a few no action was taken. But each year
> has seen more school systems making a start

toward carrying out the Court's decision. (*This Is America's Story*)

In one of the better accounts a text devotes a full page to the background of the decision and a *realistic* and *comprehensive* review of Southern resistance to it, including Governor Faubus' challenge to the federal government. It concludes:

> Other Southern states followed a policy of "token desegregation," allowing only a few Negroes to enter white schools but segregating most Negro children. By the beginning of 1961, a small portion of the three million Negro children in the South were attending integrated classes, but no legal doctrine blocked further integration. (*United States History*)

Social problems texts offer accounts that in several instances were far more *comprehensive* than those found in American histories. One of the best of these devotes three pages to the question of segregation in public schools. The points covered include: (1) tactics used by Southern school districts in avoiding desegregation, (2) the 1964 Civil Rights Act's compliance provisions, (3) 1968 statistics on school integration, (4) the 1968 Supreme Court decision on "freedom of choice" plans, (5) Northern *de facto* segregation and the reason for it, (6) reasons why *de facto* segregation is detrimental to quality education, (7) the warning of the National Advisory Commission on Civil Disorders on *de facto* segregation, (8) various solutions attempted to end *de facto* segregation, (9) the Washington, D.C., and New Rochelle, New York, federal court decisions, and (10) the desire of some black leaders for local control of schools. (*American Government*)

By contrast, two of the weakest accounts have only the following to say:

> Closely related to equal educational opportunities is the issue of Negroes and whites attending the same schools. Separating the schools on the basis of race is called *segregation*. Schools in which Negroes and whites attend the same schools are called *integrated* schools.
>
> In 1954 the United States Supreme Court stated that separate schools for Negroes were unconstitutional; they were not legal. Since then, many communities which once had segregated schools have integrated them either voluntarily or by court order. Sometimes these court orders have had to be carried out with the help of state and local police or federal troops. There are areas where segregation in schools still exists in spite of the Supreme Court decision. (*Civics for Citizens*)
>
> In 1954 Negroes gained another hard-won right when the Supreme Court ruled that compulsory segregation in public schools based on race only is a denial of equal protection under the law. During the years that followed, many school districts were made to obey this ruling. (*Civics for Americans*)

A world history which covered the Supreme Court decisions does not even hint at the resistance to the historical 1954 decision:

> The schools, however, were another matter. In many regions, especially in the South, Negroes and whites attended separate schools. Invariably the schools for the whites offered superior education, even though the legal theory

behind segregation called for "separate but equal" facilities. In 1954, the United States Supreme Court ruled that as long as educational facilities were separate, they could not really be equal. This historic decision made it necessary for all segregated school districts in the United States to end the practice as soon as possible. (*The Human Achievement*)

Black Power. While not covered by many texts, this topic is discussed in all but one of the American histories published in 1968 and 1969. Evidently the topic will be included in more books, as earlier editions are revised in the 1970's. The accounts quoted below indicate that on this topic as well accounts in the textbooks examined range from those that display *balance* and *comprehensiveness* to those that, by implication, equate Black Power with violence and thus lack *validity* and *concreteness*.

At the same time there were disagreements among Negro leaders over the future direction of the civil rights movement. Some adopted the slogan of "black power." They insisted that Negroes must secure their right to better education, decent housing, and equal job opportunities by their own efforts, rather than through working with white people. One way to reach this goal, they said, was for Negroes to use political and economic pressure. But many Negroes do not accept the idea of "black power." To them and to many white people, it seems to go too far in the direction of using force. Many people believed that "black power" contributed to outbreaks of racial violence in a number of cities during the summers of 1966 and 1967. (*This Is America's Story*)

Many whites responded to Negro rioting and the cry of "black power" by saying it was time to call a halt to the whole civil rights campaign. Some identified themselves with the so-called "white backlash." These people had accepted the earlier civil rights legislation without comment, but Negro violence prompted them to become sharp critics. In their opinion, both the Johnson administration and the civil rights revolution had gone too far. (*A History of the United States*)

Eventually, other Negro leaders defined the concept as a concentrated effort by Negroes to make the most of their numerical strength in community, state, and national decisions, particularly those most relevant to their rights and opportunities as Americans. But differences in definitions of the term led to differences among Negro leaders as to the procedures to be followed in the civil rights movement. (*Our American Nation*)

The goal now, as preached by radical leaders such as Stokely Carmichael of SNCC (Student Non-Violent Coordinating Committee), was "black power." This phrase has a variety of meanings. It may apply to organized protests against poor conditions, such as school boycotts or sit-ins by mothers on welfare. In the economic sphere it may refer to efforts by black communities to get control of their own businesses, supermarkets, and banks. It certainly means political action, defined by Carmichael as "the coming together of black people to elect representatives and *to force those representatives to speak to their needs.*" Thus the Negro began to be a force in southern politics for the first time since Reconstruction. (*History of a Free People*)

When extremists first used the term "Black Power," most Negroes and whites were deeply alarmed, taking it to be an appeal to violence. Before long, however, different groups began to define the term in their own way, and "Black Power" became a widely used rallying cry, even among black conservatives.

In economics, "Black Power" meant the growth of independent Negro business enterprises. In education, it meant local community control of schools in the ghettos. In politics, it meant the growth of political power by either the formation of a black political party or the control of politics in the ghettos through bloc voting. Socially, it meant independence from white domination, self-reliance, self-respect, and race pride. Phrases like "Black is Beautiful" and the use of terms such as "Afro-Americans" and "blacks" as well as "Black Power" came to be widely used in the Negro community. (*Rise of the American Nation*)

Civil disorder. The first two accounts quoted above draw a connection between black power and violence, an unfortunate connection that may obscure the true meaning and significance of both. By contrast, two other American histories are more frank and *valid,* having this to say about the riots that rocked the nation in the mid-1960's.

Most of the rioters were the rootless, bitter, unemployed Negroes who had had no contact with the civil rights leaders of their own race. They rebelled violently against the slum conditions that trapped them. Even though city, state, and federal government agencies tried to overcome the Negroes' despair, it persisted. . . . To help the Negroes in city slums, the civil rights crusade had to gain more than legal freedoms and equal voting rights; it also had to provide Negroes with vastly better employment opportunities. *(United States History)**

Many Americans, Negroes as well as whites, blamed the violence on a group of new and militant leaders. Whatever truth there may have been in this charge, it was by no means the whole truth. The rate of unemployment among Negroes the country over was double that of the whites, and among teenagers in Negro ghettos the rate was much higher. Even these statistics tell only part of the story, for Negroes in general worked at the lowest paying jobs. Figures on poverty released by the Social Security Administration when the rioting was at its height were revealing. In 1966 about 40 percent of the nation's nonwhites had incomes below the poverty level, as contrasted with only 11.9 percent of the whites. As the riots indicated, poverty from which there seems to be no escape is a breeding ground for violence. (*Rise of the American Nation*)

---

*Although the authors of this book give a *valid* account of the *reasons* for the riots, nevertheless the reader should note the opening sentence which describes the rioters in a manner which is somewhat inconsistent with the "Profile of a Rioter" drawn by the Report of the National Advisory Commission on Civil Disorders. See pages 128–129. The Report describes a typical rioter as underemployed, "not a migrant," "a lifelong resident of the city in which the riot took place," and "more likely to be actively engaged in civil rights efforts" than a non-rioter.

The textbook treatment of black Americans in contemporary society is a subject about which few generalizations can be made. The quality of the treatment as well as the amount varies from book to book. The only thing one can be sure of when he picks up a book that deals with American history or American government and problems is that it will most probably devote some space to the contemporary black man; how it fills that space is another question. As the excerpts above have hopefully demonstrated, a very few texts may be outstanding. Many are, at their best, bland and brief, and others, by innuendo rather than outright statements, are inaccurate and reinforce unwarranted stereotypes. Virtually none attempt to make the reader aware of what it is like to be black in our white society, poor in our affluent society, and of the close connection between blackness and poverty. However, this *can* be done. At least one social problems text explains the racial origins of much of American poverty. In addition, it makes an effort to show the student what it means to be poor in real-life situations. The following is one example of what a text can do to sensitize students to the position of many people in our contemporary society.

Case Study. An Expensive TV Set.

A door-to-door salesman who worked for a local TV store sold us a TV set, which he claimed was a new set. We didn't see the TV set until it was delivered. It played satisfactorily for about two months. When it stopped working, we called a TV repairman who said it was a reconditioned set as indicated by the "jumper on the picture tube." Upon phoning the store, we were told that the set was a new one. On the second phone call to the store we got the runaround. The manager was "out." We took the problem to the welfare worker.

Up to this time we were paying $20 a month although we received no sales contract from the salesman or the store. Each month the store mailed us a payment book, which we returned with our payment. Upon contacting the store manager, the welfare worker was told that the set was new. The storekeeper agreed to come over and look at the set, but he never showed up.

The welfare worker advised us to write a letter saying that the store would get no further payments unless "some sort of satisfactory arrangement is made." We never got an answer to our letter, and we made no payments for about six months. The store went bankrupt and turned its accounts over to another furniture company. The new store said: "If you pay all your back payments, we'll send out a repairman and nothing more." Two weeks later my husband's salary was garnisheed (taken legally for non-payment of a debt). My husband did not get a chance to appear in court. He received no summons or anything. They just sent the garnishment to his employer. He found out his salary was garnisheed when his boss called him in and said, "Straighten this out or else you're fired." (*Problems of Democracy*)

In contrast to the above attempt at making students aware of the difficulties of many people in our nation, one text captions a photograph taken in the kitchen of a black family this way:

Not all homes can be as modern and attractive as this one, but all can be made comfortable, and life in them relaxed, friendly, and enjoyable, regardless of income. (*Building Citizenship*)

To imply that all black people in this country can be comfortable and relaxed regardless of their income is as great a breach of the criterion of *realism* as any found by this study. Most probably the statement was made in all innocence; however, that in itself is telling. If those responsible for the compiling of textbooks are themselves unaware of the reality of a situation, how can they hope to convey it to their young readers?

B. HISTORICAL REFERENCES

The earlier ADL study found that: "Despite a growing need for students to understand the role of Negro Americans in our increasingly integrated nation, textbooks continue to present a picture of this group primarily as slaves and as inexperienced, exploited, ignorant freedmen. Few texts make an effort to redress this imbalance by carrying the story into the present century. Even where some material appears on post-1876 progress and contributions of Negroes, it is usually insufficient in scope and depth to counteract the textbook stereotype of a simple, inferior people."[*]

Both quantitative and qualitative changes are immediately apparent in the texts examined a decade later. Fewer of them contain descriptions of blacks that reinforce old stereotypes. More accurate and balanced information is provided about blacks in both the slavery and the Reconstruction periods. More

---

[*]ADL Study, p. 43.

texts offer accounts of black Americans after 1876. Yet all the texts fail to include many relevant references to black Americans, especially for the years between 1876 and 1954. Furthermore, not all texts avoid statements that could reinforce invalid stereotypes. In sum, dramatic changes have taken place in the treatment of this topic. However, most textbooks still fall short of giving the black man his due representation.

Of the thirty American and world histories examined, few can be considered completely adequate in their coverage of black history. Since it is impossible, in these few pages, to include all or even a majority of textbook references to black people, only a few typical examples will be presented. The reader who wishes to pursue this subject in greater depth may consult a study done by Irving Sloan for the American Federation of Teachers, entitled *The Negro in Modern American History Textbooks*. This study, revised in 1968, reviews nearly all references to black Americans made in twenty-three American histories, including twelve examined and reported on here. Other studies are also available which analyze how individual texts have treated this topic, including one by Mark M. Krug (referred to later in this chapter) that contrasts textbook treatments with primary historical sources relevant to the topics reviewed.

If one begins at the beginning, one would expect to find some references to the cultural origins of the black people who were brought to America. After all, the origins of the English colonists are usually laid out in great detail. However, such is not the case with the black man. Only two American histories offer any references to his origins. One of these contains a lengthy account, from which the following passages are taken:

> Long before the New World was discovered, a number of African societies—among them the West African kingdoms, or empires, of Ghana, Melle, and Songhay—had attained a high degree of civilization. For example, the ancient empire of Ghana, from which the modern nation of Ghana has taken its name, flourished for centuries. It reached the peak of its power five hundred years before Columbus discovered America. Under the Negro king, Askia the Great, the two cities of Jenné (je-NAY) and Timbuktu became commercial and intellectual centers whose fame spread to Spain, North Africa, and the Middle East. Moslem businessmen, statesmen, and scholars traveled to the cities of this African empire regularly. At the same time scholars from the university located at Timbuktu won fame for their intellectual activities. They visited and served as professors at the universities of Fez, Tunis, and Cairo.

> Another example of a high level of development was the Ashanti (ah • SHAN • ti) kingdom on the Gold Coast. When the first British mission visited the Ashanti capital in 1817, the Britishers were astonished to see the level of culture the Negroes had established. The Britishers saw a well-organized society with trained soldiers and an elaborate social life. They saw the high craftsmanship of the Negroes revealed in beautifully woven silk robes and skillfully fashioned jewelry.

> The first European visitors found similar

conditions in the kingdom of Dahomey (dah-HOH-mi). There roads were broad, clean, well laid out; buildings clean and neat. Law and order prevailed. Trade prospered. Taxes and custom duties were collected. A courier service was in operation. Wood carving had reached an advanced stage of development.

Africans from kingdoms and empires such as these, as well as men and women from the most primitive tribes, were torn from their homes and families. (*Rise of the American Nation*)

Two other American history references to cultural backgrounds are too brief and perfunctory to have meaning for the student. One of these merely asks the question, "How much of their former rich African culture did the Negroes retain in America?" (*History of a Free People*). Unfortunately, details of that culture are not given. Yet all three of these are positive references and, in fact, the only ones on the topic to be offered by fifteen texts. World histories would be expected to do more, but only six actually meet the criterion of *inclusion* by presenting such material and in only two cases is it lengthy and informative. The fact is that twenty-seven out of thirty histories fail to meet the criterion of *comprehensiveness* on this topic and twenty-one the criterion of *inclusion* as well.

Another topic of interest is how and when the black man came to America. With the exception of one account of a black sailing with Columbus *(History: U.S.A.)*, the texts do not refer to the fact that the first blacks came here with the Spanish explorers and that their presence therefore predates that of the English colonists. However, all but two

American hisories do tell the story of the arrival of blacks in Jamestown in 1619. One of the briefest of these accounts states:

> In 1619 a Dutch ship landed twenty Negroes at Jamestown, Virginia. It seems that some of these Negroes were sold to local planters—not as slaves but as servants, who after serving for a few years would be freed. Slowly, however, permanent bondage replaced temporary servitude, and more Negroes were brought to the colonies as slaves. (*History of Our United States*)

Another account does more than simply state that the first blacks were not slaves. It compared them to the

> . . . thousands of men and women from Europe [who] worked as servants for a period of years to pay for their transportation. Once they had repaid the debt, they settled on their own land and worked for themselves. By the 1640's, however, Africans were being brought to the British colonies as slaves. (*Rise of the American Nation*)

Accounts like these present a positive image of the black American and indicate that he was not qualified for slavery by some inherent attribute. However, not all the texts reflect current scholarship as do the two quoted above. A few, as in the passage below, state that the first blacks in America were slaves:

> An historic event occurred in 1619, when a Dutch war vessel sailed into port with 20 Negroes aboard, who were sold as slaves. It was some time, however, before Negro slaves were

used in great numbers. (*The Making of Modern America*)

Only a few of the texts reviewed meet the criteria of *realism* or *comprehensiveness* by including discussions of the horror of the slave trade itself. Two of these accounts follow:

Description of a Slave Ship.

This passage describes the conditions on a slave ship captured in 1829. The same words could have been written about such vessels in earlier periods, including the colonial years.

"But the circumstance which struck us most forcibly was how it was possible for such a number of human beings to exist, packed up and wedged together as tight as they could cram, in low cells three feet high, the greater part of which, except that immediately under the grated hatchways, was shut out from light or air, and this when the thermometer, exposed to the open sky, was standing in the shade, on our deck, at 89°. The space between decks was divided into two compartments 3 feet 3 inches high; the size of one was 16 feet by 18 and of the other 40 by 21; into the first were crammed the women and girls, into the second the men and boys: 226 fellow creatures were thus thrust into one space 288 feet square and 336 into another space 800 feet square, giving to the whole an average of 23 inches and to each of the women not more than 13 inches. We also found manacles and fetters of different kinds, but it appears that they had all been taken off before we boarded." (*Our American Nation*)

The slave trade that furnished Negroes to American markets was a horrible example of man's inhumanity to man. It has been estimated that about 30 per cent of the Negroes put on shipboard in Africa died crossing the Atlantic, it being a common practice to throw the sick overboard. Probably half the survivors died soon after reaching America, because of strange food and diseases for which they had built up no immunity. (*History of a Free People*)

Stereotyping statements continue to exist in textbooks, although not to as great an extent as in the past. One passage that was criticized in 1960 is still included in the 1966 edition of that text. It describes the Ku Klux Klan as being effective in arousing "the superstitions of the uneducated Negroes" (*The Making of Modern America*). The terms *superstition* and *uneducated* contribute to the image of a simple, inferior people which most textbooks had previously conveyed.

In many ways a text can inadvertently reinforce stereotypes of black men as a simple people incapable of helping themselves. Notice that in the following passages blacks are shown only as persons receiving help from their usual protectors, Northerners and the federal government. A balanced account would also include the efforts of the blacks themselves in resisting the Klan:

The Ku Klux Klan was the most active of the societies. Its purpose was to frighten the freedmen so that they would not vote for or support the carpetbag governments. Clad in ghostly white hoods and robes, Klan members rode silently around the countryside in the dead of

night, terrifying Negroes by their threats. All
too often, when their warnings were not
heeded, the Klan members returned and used
violence. The Ku Klux Klan succeeded so well
in frightening the Negroes that Congress ordered federal soldiers to break up the organization. (*This Is America's Story*)

The Klan was the most powerful. Dressed
in sheets and hoods, Klansmen appeared at
Negroes' homes by night and warned the occupants not to vote.

As the Klan grew in numbers, it grew bold-
er. Threats against Negroes turned into violence. Members of the Klan, and other secret
societies, did terrible things to their opponents,
especially to the Negroes. Northerners demanded that Congress step in and protect the
Negroes' right to vote. The Fifteenth Amend-
ment was added to the Constitution. (*History
of Our United States*)

The history of the Reconstruction period shows
some of the most flagrant abuses in textbook treatment. Stereotyping is common, although progress
has been made in recent years. Mark Krug, a
renowned professor of education specializing in
Civil War and Reconstruction history, stresses the
stereotyping which exists in textbooks. The sup-
posed "inability" of blacks to govern, he states, leads
to written history that is riddled with inaccuracies.
The ignorance of blacks is linked to the greed and
selfishness of the Carpetbaggers. In a *School Review*
article, Krug uses *This Is America's Story* to make
his point cogently:

The Reconstruction governments are called
"Carpetbag Governments." . . . The authors

have no compunctions about revealing their disapproval of the Reconstruction Acts and the Fourteenth and Fifteenth Amendments which gave the right to vote to blacks.*

This kind of stereotyping is frequently seen in many secondary school textbooks. The improvements that have occurred in no way justify the inaccuracy of much of the treatment of Reconstruction.

This section has presented examples from some areas in which texts should give information about black people. As has been noted, not all—or even, in some cases, many—texts cover these points, and of those that meet the criterion of *inclusion,* some do so in an inaccurate and misleading manner. After a review of other historical references to blacks in the textbooks examined, it seems that the findings presented above are representative of the general nature of coverage in this area. On the whole, textbook publishers have dramatically improved their fare, but the improvement has been awkward and uneven.

This review has noted an increase in the number of historical references, but, as the examples above indicate, the quality of individual textbook accounts varies. Some are inadequate, while others are both competent and creative. All texts now mention and picture certain outstanding black Americans, but some are too perfunctory in this practice. Many more texts than previously now discuss the black man in the Civil War; yet only one mentions black contributions in the Revolutionary War. All texts in-

---

*Mark M. Krug, "Freedom and Racial Equality: A Study of 'Revised' High School History Texts," *School Review,* May 1970, pp. 297–354.

clude some information about the black man in the
period between Reconstruction and World War II.
But only if all the different pieces of information
presented by each of the fifteen American histories
reviewed are put together do they present the total
picture that each text should individually present.
For example, only two texts tell about the race riots
in the summer of 1919, when twenty-five Northern
cities were shaken by riots. True, many texts contain accounts of slavery that stand in stark contrast
to earlier treatments. In some texts, however, accounts of slavery are still biased, presenting an *unrealistic* and somewhat romanticized view.

Dramatic improvement has certainly taken place,
but it is significant primarily in contrast to the kind
of information found in texts ten years ago. It seems
reasonable to judge that today the treatment of the
black man in most social studies textbooks is still far
from adequate. Of the thirty histories examined, less
than one-third could be considered as adequate for
use in a school classroom where complete and un-
biased coverage of the topic is a goal. To expect
more texts to deserve this judgment may be folly. It
is apparent that textbook authors and publishers
supply what the market demands. While no evidence
of an earlier practice of publishing regional editions
of the same text was found, it is worthwhile to note
that not only one of the least adequate books examined, but also one of the best, is distributed by the
same publisher. The negatively evaluated text was
selected for review in 1960 as well as for the present
study because of its popularity. It has changed little,
if at all. If it continues to be popular, one cannot
help wondering whether there will be any change in
future editions.

C. THE NATURE OF RACE

The 1960 report found that scientific facts about race rarely appeared in social studies texts. As Marcus emphasized, experts in intergroup relations have repeatedly stated that such facts can help dispel false beliefs about the alleged inferiority of black people. Yet at that time not one of the twenty-four texts scrutinized stated that Negroes and Caucasians have the same inherent potentialities. Today the odds have not changed much. Only three of forty-five texts state flatly that race is not a factor in the determination of intelligence, and one other implies that whites are not inherently superior. The more typical treatment of race consists of a labeling, usually by color, of the three major groups of mankind. Yet even at this level, the subject is covered by only thirteen of the forty-five texts examined—nine of them being world histories and the other four social problems texts. And of the thirteen texts that do discuss race, only six either state or imply that there are no "pure" races.

Of the forty-five texts examined, thirty-two fail to meet the criterion of *inclusion*. Furthermore, of those that do, only three approach the criteria of *comprehensiveness* and *balance*. Most typically, references to race are similar to those in the following brief passages, from a world history and a civics text, respectively.

> *The world's races*. The world's population of about three billion people is divided into more or less distinct groups called races. We are not yet sure how they originated. Racial differences are based on physical traits, of which the most prominent is skin color. There are three main races, generally called Negroid,

Mongoloid, and Caucasoid. We also use color labels—black, yellow, and white—as convenient, though less accurate terms. *(The Record of Mankind)*

All human beings belong to the same biological species. Therefore, "race" is a term or expression used to identify subgroups of the species with similar genetic and physical qualities. The three major "races" are Caucasoid, or white; Negro, or black; and Mongoloid, or yellow. All of these groups include many examples of intermingling. *(Building Citizenship)*

As to the question of the purity of the racial groups, the following is the strongest statement made by those textbooks that do not consider the relationship between race and intelligence.

The myth of racial purity—At this point we should note that just as there are no pure nations, so there are no pure races. Many people believe that at one time pure race did exist and that in recent centuries they have become mixed by intermarriage. This belief lacks support from science. Instead, most scientists agree that the different races descended from a common stock, and that all mankind belongs to the same species, *Homo sapiens,* as we have seen. *(A Global History of Man)*

Most statements hedge the issue, as in the following passages.

Scientists say that among all members of the human race there are more similarities than there are differences. *(Our World Through the Ages)*

[Some] scientists have classified human beings into three major races. . . . Other scientists have recognized six major races. Still others, because of the lack of clear-cut differences among the groups and because of the great variation within each group, have advocated that the term "race" be abandoned entirely. *(New Dimensions of World History)*

Competent authorities agree that there are few pure racial groups remaining today, because mixture of the races has been so widespread. Intermingling of races is the result of conquest, migration, the sale of slaves, intermarriage, trade relations, and colonization. *(The Challenge of Democracy)*

Nevertheless three texts (two world histories and one social problems book) satisfy the criteria with their treatment of this topic, thus demonstrating that it is possible for a textbook to integrate the scientific facts of race, as they are known today, into its material. The best and most extensive of these treatments is from a social problems text. Below is a portion of that discussion:

Upon what do scientists agree? In the summer of 1950 an international panel of scientists was gathered together by the United Nations Educational, Scientific, and Cultural Organization. The UNESCO biologists, geneticists, psychologists, sociologists, and anthropologists issued a "Statement on Race." Their statement summarizes the points on which modern scientists are generally agreed, as follows:

The one trait which above all others has been significant in the development of men's mental capacities has been the ability to learn.

It has made for great flexibility and adaptability in human development, and it is a trait which human beings of all races, all creeds, and all nations possess.

Race is more a social myth than a biological fact. The intermingling of peoples throughout countless centuries has destroyed any possibility of a so-called "pure" race. As a social myth, said the scientists, race "has created an enormous amount of human and social damage. In recent years it has taken a heavy toll in human lives and caused untold suffering. It still prevents the normal development of millions of human beings and deprives civilization of the effective cooperation of productive minds."

The range of mental capacities in all races is much the same. There is no available scientific proof that the groups of mankind differ significantly in intelligence, temperament, or other inborn mental characteristics. Given similar degrees of cultural (particularly educational) opportunities to realize their potentialities, the average achievement of the members of each major racial group is about the same.

No large modern national or religious group is a race. Nor are people who speak a single language, or live in a single geographical area, or share in a single cultural community necessarily a race. As for personality and character traits, these may be considered raceless. In every human group, said the scientists, "a rich variety of personality and character types will be found, and there is no reason for believing that any human group is richer than any other in these respects."

Here, then, are several important conclusions about men of all races and creeds. Study them, think about them, discuss them with others; try to understand them fully. Seek further information about these conclusions from reliable sources. (*Problems of Democracy*)

D. INTEGRATED ILLUSTRATIONS OF AMERICAN LIFE

In 1960 the findings in this area were these:

> On the whole, textbook illustrations do not reflect an increasingly integrated, interracial American society. No photograph of Negro and white Americans together in any situation is to be found in the eight American histories. Among the eight world histories, only one contains interracial photographs. . . . Only two of the eight social-problems texts include similar illustrations.*

This is no longer true. Nearly all the texts examined contained photographs of integrated subject matter. Those that did not were often, but not always, world histories that devoted little space to contemporary American life. In a few cases the quantity and quality of such illustrations was quite outstanding. One American history even used integrated drawings when photographs were not available. It is a great change from the textbooks of the past to see black scientists, doctors, researchers, pedestrians, policemen, nurses, students, executives, statesmen and boy scouts in interaction with their white colleagues. It is especially encouraging to see all this and more in the same textbook, as in one civics text.

Furthermore, in most instances the illustrations do

---

*ADL Study, p. 47.

not reinforce historical stereotypes. Blacks are shown supervising whites, managing clean and beautiful homes, getting marriage licenses, and engaged in pursuits common to all Americans. However, while most books do contain some integrated photographs, the number of them must be increased considerably to reflect accurately our society.

Another improvement that should be noted is that, in addition to their integrated illustrations, almost all texts do contain photographs that focus on outstanding black Americans. Men such as Dr. Martin Luther King, Jr., Thurgood Marshall, Frederick Douglass, Robert Weaver, and Ralph Bunche appear repeatedly in the textbooks examined, and this list could be lengthened. Certainly one positive statement that must be made about the textbooks examined is that black Americans are pictured and featured with greater frequency and dignity than ever before. What remains now is for *all* texts to follow their lead in eradicating false illusions of an all-white America.

SUMMARY

When compared against the findings of past reports, the treatment of black Americans in the secondary school social studies textbooks examined in 1969 has these characteristics:

A. No longer is the black man's position in contemporary American society largely ignored. Yet the tendency to treat racial inequality and attempts at its eradication with complacent generalizations rather than with concrete facts continues in a significant majority of texts. In too many books the discussion of Supreme Court decisions and Congressional legislation still bypasses any consideration of the principles underlying them and of subsequent ongoing attempts at both compliance and evasion. However, the achievements of living black Americans are mentioned more frequently than in the past.

B. Many historical facts relevant to black people continue to be ignored. While the historical portrayal of blacks as simple, childlike slaves and uneducated, bewildered freedmen is no longer the general practice, material that perpetuates these stereotypes continues to exist in individual texts. Moreover, a vast majority continue to neglect most aspects of black history between the years 1876 and 1954. Although references to outstanding blacks in American history abound, these are not sufficient to counterbalance the failure of many texts to integrate relevant aspects of the black American heritage into their accounts of American history. Furthermore, these texts also fail to convey to the student the rich native African heritage of black people.

C. The scientific knowledge underlying a sound understanding of the basic similarity and equality of all of mankind continues to be absent from the great majority of the textbooks. Thus they still fail to meet their responsibilities in contributing to healthy intergroup relations and the eradication of prejudicial beliefs.

D. In most instances textbooks no longer portray America as an all-white nation. Photographs and illustrations are used to depict this land as an increasingly integrated one, although few textbooks do this to the extent demanded by the reality of the situation. In addition, most texts feature illustrations of outstanding black Americans.

CHAPTER FOUR

TEXTBOOK TREATMENT OF OTHER MINORITIES IN AMERICA

The American Council on Education study in 1949 made the following observations concerning textbook presentations of American Indians, Oriental Americans, and Spanish-speaking Americans:

A. Only two major attitudes governed the treatment of American Indians. The first was that of cruel, bloodthirsty Indians whose rights were unquestionably superseded by the interests of white pioneers. The second was that of the noble redskin, a high-minded son of nature. Almost without exception, no convincing picture of Indians as a group, or of the cultural characteristics of Indian life, past or present, was presented.

B. Asiatic minorities, such as those of Chinese and Japanese origin or descent, were frequently treated in a manner implying they were racially inferior. Offensive generalizations were applied to such groups, and positive material about their current status and contributions was omitted.

C. The Spanish-speaking peoples of the United States were generally ignored; if not, they were sometimes dealt with in terms likely to intensify prevalent stereotypes.

While the ADL study of 1960 did not examine textbook treatment of the American Indians, in its review of twenty-four social studies textbooks, it found that treatment of Orientals and Spanish-speaking Americans had not changed since the 1949

112

report. In this section of our present study attention is once again directed at assessing the efforts of social studies textbooks to portray positively the characteristics and contributions of these groups to our pluralistic culture.

A. THE AMERICAN INDIAN

Those criticisms expressed in the 1949 report, regarding textbook treatment of the American Indian seem no longer applicable. Although the historical references to Indians emphasize periods of struggle and warfare, these are counterbalanced by (1) the tone of the presentations themselves, which frequently show the deceit of the white man and the justice of the Indian's struggle and (2) frequent references to the civilization and culture of the Indians and their contributions to American progress. However, on this topic there remains much room for improvement in textbooks in general.

Of the forty-five textbooks examined, seventeen make no reference to the American Indian whatever. Ten of those that fail to meet the criterion of *inclusion* are world histories, and seven are social problems texts. Of the books that do discuss the Indians, two world histories and three social problems texts offer only brief and perfunctory information. Therefore, of the thirty texts in these categories only three world histories and five social problems texts can be considered reasonably adequate by the criteria of *inclusion, comprehensiveness,* and *balance.* As an example of the brevity and inadequacy of some treatments, consider the following complete accounts from a world history and a social problems text, respectively.

> War paint and tomahawk, colorful feather headdresses, and blankets of many patterns

made up the costume of the American Indian. In western cowboy stories and television plays, the Indian often plays the part of the villain and sometimes the part of the hero.

The North American Indian's civilization was very simple. The Mayas of Central America, the Aztecs of Mexico, and the Incas of Peru were more advanced peoples and their civilizations were superior to those farther north. (*The Pageant of World History*)

The Indian Problem. Another group of people who have suffered at the hands of the government are the Indians. The Indians were the first Americans, but none of us can feel proud of the treatment that has been accorded them. Our ancestors took their land from them and drove them from their hunting grounds. Over the years, our government made many agreements and treaties with them, but these were often broken.

In recent years the government has tried to make up for the past ill treatment. Today most Indians live on reservations, special land set aside for them. These reservations, which cover about 30,000,000 acres of land, are chiefly in the Southwest. In 1924 Congress granted citizenship to all native-born Indians. The Federal government through its Bureau of Indian Affairs maintains about 200 schools for them. Today Indians are encouraged to leave their reservations and live as other Americans do. When they do, they have some of the same difficulties that other minority groups face. (*Civics for Americans*)

As compared with world history and social problems texts, American histories do much better. As one would expect, all of them discuss American Indians. However, in contrast to past practices, nearly all these presentations point out the deceitful, evil practices used by the new Americans on the Indians. Passages like the following are the rule rather than the exception:

> The ways of the white man made little appeal to a people used to the freedom of a nomadic life. Since it was impossible for the Indians to stop the advance of the Europeans, their conquest was only a matter of time. But the merciless way in which the Indians were enslaved, massacred, driven from their hunting grounds, and cheated by the white man is a chapter of dishonor. (*Our American Republic*)

> *The government moves the Indians to reservations.* The government's Indian policies proved to be neither realistic nor humane. By the 1850's it had become clear that the Plains were not a "Great American Desert," as had once been thought. Someday the white man would want to claim that useful land from the Indians. The government, therefore, forced the Plains Indians to sign treaties which set off large areas called *reservations* for the Indians' use. Since the Indians were confined within the boundaries of the reservations, they had to abandon their old ways of hunting. The government agreed to supply the Indians on reservations with food and clothing, but by the 1870's corruption was widespread in every phase of the government's Indian policy. Spoiled meat and moth-eaten blankets were

distributed to the Indians, and unscrupulous traders found ways to sell forbidden liquor to them. Moreover, the government violated its treaties with the Indians. The reservations were constantly reduced in size for the benefit of the miners, ranchers, or farmers who wanted the land. (*A History of the United States*)

The Indian Problem. You have perhaps discovered by now that the land taken over from the Indian tribes was not always won in a clean, fair way. Earlier chapters have told how, at various times, representatives of our government secured Indian lands by treaty. The Indians were told to move farther west and promised that they would be left in peace. But always the pioneer's hunger for land, and the urge to move westward, drove him to break his agreements with the Indians and push them on to some other place. Who can blame the proud Indian chiefs and warriors for trying to keep for themselves and their families some part of their native land on which to live? (*History of Our United States*)

The text from which the last account above is taken uses the opportunity its discussion provides to ask the student, "What people in our day have claimed the right to overrun another nation and take whatever they wanted?" This is an excellent two-way approach to emphasizing lessons history offers us today and also to making the past more vivid by relating it to the student's present-day experience. In addition to pointing out the problems the white man brought the Indian, these texts frequently discuss the varied cultures and contributions of the Indians.

One of the briefer accounts is the following from a "Focus" section of an American history text:

> *A Legacy from the Indians.*
>
> The value of the contribution the American Indians have made to the world is beyond reckoning. Mankind will be forever in their debt.
>
> Nearly five hundred years have passed since men and women from the Old World began to settle the American continents. During all that time, none of the settlers nor their descendants have discovered and developed a single major agricultural product from the wild trees and plants of the New World. And yet, long before the first Europeans landed on the shores of the Americas, the Indians had developed more than twenty valuable products. In addition, they had learned to use many other products of the forests and grasslands. The amazing truth is that more than half of all the agricultural goods produced in the world today came from plants originally discovered and cultivated by American Indians.
>
> The shelves of our stores are filled with these products, either in their natural form or processed into an almost endless variety of packaged and canned goods. How different our eating habits would be if we did not have corn, tomatoes, white and sweet potatoes, and the many varieties of beans! If we did not have peanuts, chestnuts, pumpkins, strawberries, blackberries, blueberries, cranberries, and crab apples! If we did not have chocolate and maple syrup! If we did not have turkeys! (*Rise of the American Nation*)

Eleven texts—seven American histories and four world histories—give substance to their accounts of the Indian's presence in America by relating the theory which suggests how they migrated here from Asia centuries ago across the Bering Strait.

The major failing of most histories is that they do not discuss the Indian in contemporary times. Only five do this, but for the most part either in passing references or in accounts that fail to measure up to the criterion of *realism* by omitting any mention of the poverty in which most Indians now live. Below is an example of an account that completely neglects the reality of the Indian's present-day plight:

> *The Indians Today.* Today over 520,000 Indians live in the United States. There are about 100 reservations in the country, most under the supervision of the Bureau of Indian Affairs, a part of the Department of the Interior. The bureau is directed by a Commissioner of Indian Affairs.
>
> Indians do not have to live on these reservations, but many prefer to do so because they pay no tax on the land, and because they like living among themselves. Indians who live on reservations farm or raise livestock. Others work in the cities, and the Bureau of Indian Affairs helps them to find jobs and living quarters.
>
> The tribes are still important to the Indian, and self-government within them is supported by the United States government. The tribes elect officers, punish minor offenses, borrow money from the federal government, and lend money to their members. Today, like any other

citizens, Indians may vote. *(History of Our United States)*

To find a reasonably full account of the Indians in contemporary society we must turn to the social problems texts. Six of these cover the topic but only one deals frankly with the problems currently facing these people. The other accounts are merely brief references or statistical treatments under the topic "Bureau of Indian Affairs." With the exception of a fully satisfactory treatment in only one book the only inkling a student can get that the life of the Indians is not always a happy one is from these two brief passages in two different social problems texts:

> Still . . . the Indian's lot remains a far from happy one. After one exhaustive survey of the Bureau's work in 1966, the Senate Interior Committee declared that "Indians remain at the bottom of the economic ladder, have the highest rate of unemployment, and suffer chronic poverty." It directed the Bureau to "redouble its efforts" in order that Indians may soon "take their long-awaited, rightful place in our national life." *(Magruder's American Government)*

> The Bureau of Indian Affairs has been carrying out a voluntary relocation program since 1951. Its purpose is to aid Indians to find good jobs and to make adjustments to modern living conditions. While some Indians have been helped to make this adjustment, others are unhappy and ultimately drift back to their old environment. *(The Challenge of Democracy)*

By contrast, the one treatment to fulfill the criteria of *realism* and *comprehensiveness* devotes four pages to the American Indian's problems today and to developments that are now taking place. Compare the introductory paragraphs of that discussion with the passages quoted above:

> *American Indian problems today.* About 550,000 Indians live in the United States at the present time. All are full citizens of the United States and, in theory at least, have the right to vote. Many have served with distinction in our military services in recent wars. Nearly one third mingle with the general population, some in poverty and some in reasonably prosperous adjustment to the white man's way of life. About two thirds live on reservations and are served by the Bureau of Indian Affairs. Most reservations are in the West and Southwest with the largest in Oklahoma, Arizona, New Mexico and South Dakota.
>
> Reservation lands are generally poor and incapable of supporting the rapidly growing Indian population. Poverty on many reservations is appalling. About half the labor force is unemployed. Average income is half of what the government considers as poverty level. The infant mortality rate is 70 per cent higher than the United States average. More than 90 per cent of Indian homes are substandard, and half are one or two rooms built by their occupants with any available materials. Adults over 45 have an average of five years of school. Adults under 45 average eight years. (*Problems of Democracy*)

Although the textbook treatment of the American Indian has changed dramatically since 1949, efforts and demands for better handling of this topic should not cease. Accounts of the Indian's place in contemporary society must offer *balance* and *comprehensiveness*. And while we are encouraged by the many fine discussions of the history of American Indians, there are still a few that appear to come directly from the Wild West. As an example, consider a reference to Indians as "some red men" (*History of Our United States*) and a section heading which reads: "The danger from hostile Indians was removed" (*United States History*). Happily these are, for once, the exception rather than the norm. But even the exception should cease.

B. AMERICANS OF ORIENTAL DESCENT

The 1960 report had these comments to make concerning textbook treatments of our citizens of Oriental background:

> Not one book among the 24 contains a diversified, balanced portrayal of Chinese Americans or Japanese Americans. Characteristics such as the strong family unit, reverence for tradition, low rates of juvenile delinquency and crime, and industriousness of many members of this group continue to go unmentioned. Instead, a sense of racial inferiority pervades American history accounts of cheap labor, starvation wages, and popular demand for restriction or exclusion in the late nineteenth century. In terms of occupation, the first Chinese railroad laborers and the later laundrymen and cooks are given no contemporary successors, such as

engineers, teachers, doctors, and businessmen.*

The present 1969 study is unable to report any
significant changes in textbook presentations of this
topic. Not one world history makes any overt reference to the presence of people of Oriental origin
in the United States. Of the thirty American history
and American problems and civics texts analyzed,
two histories and eight problems and civics texts
violate the criterion of *inclusion* by totally failing to
mention this minority group. Furthermore, of the
eleven American histories and five social problems
texts that mention Chinese Americans, and of the
ten American histories and six social problems texts
that mention Japanese Americans, none meets the
dual criteria of *comprehensiveness* and *balance*. As
a matter of fact, only two textbooks make references
to either Chinese or Japanese Americans in contemporary society, and these are hardly to be considered
complete. The following constitutes the sum total of
those references:

> Since China was one of the Allies during
> World War II, much of the feeling against the
> Chinese in America has subsided. Nevertheless,
> there still remains some discrimination against
> them. The younger generation is rapidly be-
> coming Americanized through education. The
> Chinese still meet obstacles when they try to
> enter some of the better occupations or when
> they attempt to move into certain neighbor-
> hoods, but they are gradually getting away
> from the sheltered life of Chinese communi-
> ties. (*The Challenge of Democracy*)

---

*ADL Study, p. 53.

Since World War II, when China was one of our allies, much of the prejudice against Chinese-Americans has vanished. Today the younger generation is rapidly becoming Americanized. Many Chinese-Americans have distinguished themselves in the sciences and professional fields. . . .

Today more than 80 per cent of the Japanese-Americans in the United States live in the West, particularly in California. Many also live in Hawaii. One study of this group concludes that the highly educated Japanese-Americans who resettled outside the western part of the United States moved into better jobs than they had formerly been able to obtain. Those who returned to the West, the report says, were still in a markedly disadvantaged occupational position compared to the white majority although some have improved their economic and social status markedly. Therefore much remains to be accomplished in improving race relations. (*Problems of Democracy*)

With the exception of the above accounts and two photographs—one of the Chinese physicist Tsung-dao Lee (*Our American Nation*) and one of the Japanese architect Minoru Yamasaki (*A High School History of Modern America*)—there were found no other references to contemporary Oriental Americans in the texts examined.

In almost all instances, presentations of Chinese Americans in textbooks are used either to explain how immigration laws of exclusion came into being or in reference to the building of the railroads in the West. Typically these passages were similar to the following, from an American history and an American problems text, respectively:

> *Limits are placed upon the number of immigrants.* As a result of these fears a cry arose that immigration should be restricted. Even as early as 1882 a law had been passed which forbade the immigration of Chinese laborers. Californians, in particular, objected to letting in Chinese, as well as Japanese, because they were willing to work for low wages. From time to time other laws were made restricting immigration. In 1917, for example, a law was passed barring immigrants who could not read. Then in 1924 a law limiting immigration in general was passed. This law forbade most immigration from Asian countries and limited the number of other newcomers to about 150,000 a year. (*This Is America's Story*)

> *Restriction of immigration.* Soon after gold was discovered in California, Chinese workers came to this country in great numbers. The Chinese were willing to do the hard labor in mines, on ranches, and in railroad construction. At first these laborers were welcome. Then hard times came. Sometimes Americans were out of work, while the Chinese were employed because they would work longer hours for less pay. Consequently, in 1882, Congress passed laws which excluded Chinese immigrants for 10 years. The law was extended later and became permanent until War War II. (*Civics for Americans*)

Most frequently, accounts in American history texts continue to deserve the 1960 criticism, which stated: "Because this factor [economic competition] is not counterbalanced with positive information about these people either then or now, the impression is created of a flood of justly-resented, 'cut-rate-labor' intruders"* Two accounts directly criticized in the 1960 study are retained in the later editions of the same texts analyzed for the present study. One tells readers that "the Chinese coolies . . . worked for starvation wages and lived under conditions that Americans would not endure" (*The Making of Modern America*). The following, as the 1960 report pointed out, offers an explanation that is more *concrete* but tends to reinforce an outdated stereotype through lack of *balance* and *comprehensiveness.*

> The Chinese were welcomed. They found jobs as cooks and laundrymen, and they also helped to build the Central Pacific Railroad eastward across the Rocky Mountains.
>
> Because the Chinese had been brought up in the terrible poverty of their own country, they were willing to work in America for wages on which other workers could not live. When Americans began to fill up California, they objected to further Chinese immigration because the Chinese worked for such low wages. . . . In 1882, the United States government passed a law forbidding Chinese workers to enter the United States. *(Story of the American Nation)*

Still another account may reinforce stereotyped images of the Chinese as a reclusive group unwilling and unable to be assimilated into American life.

> Unemployment mounted in California as in

---

*ADL Study, p. 53.

other parts of the United States. Men feared
that the Chinese would take their jobs at low
wages. Fear and insecurity were increased because the Chinese, for reasons not always of
their own choosing, lived entirely to themselves, and did not learn American ways.
(*Rise of the American Nation*)

Accounts like these two, which may be based on
historical fact, should be balanced by other equally
factual accounts that reflect the positive attributes of
our citizens of Chinese background.

On the other hand, most references to Japanese
Americans continue to offer "positive—and even
provocative—intergroup material."* Fourteen of the
fifteen texts with textual material on Japanese
Americans deal with either their internment during
World War II or the valor and loyalty of the "Nisei"
troops that served in that war. Several of these accounts even express indignation at the confinement
of the Japanese Americans and stress the fact that
their loyalty was never disproved. Some of the finer
examples of this treatment follow:

> . . . on one important occasion the rights of
> civilians were violated by the federal govern-
> ment on a scale never before seen. In the ex-
> citement following the attack on Pearl Harbor,
> over a hundred thousand Japanese-Americans,
> most of them citizens, were routed from their
> homes and herded into detention camps. It is
> estimated that they lost nearly half their prop-
> erty. That this forced "relocation" was unnec-
> essary was revealed by the loyalty of Japanese-
> Americans in Hawaii during the war, as well

---
*ADL Study, p. 54.

as by the fine fighting record of Nisei (Japanese-American) troops. (*History of a Free People*)

After Japan attacked Pearl Harbor, a wave of war hysteria, based on rumors and anti-Japanese sentiments, spread throughout the West Coast. Fearful of sabotage and espionage in case the Japanese forces attacked our Western cities, the military command of the district ordered the removal of the Japanese from the coastal areas on the grounds of "military necessity." Nearly 110,000 of them were removed to relocation centers. The Japanese who were uprooted were compelled to abandon their property and to sell personal effects for what they would bring on the open market. Suddenly being deprived of earning power, the Japanese were unable to continue payments on insurance policies, mortgages, or installment debts. Much valuable property was lost through foreclosure, repossession, and cancellation of contracts. Naturally, these citizens were bitter because they had committed no criminal offense. Furthermore, no Nisei was ever found guilty of disloyalty to this country; yet they were denied the constitutional privileges which would protect their property. Nor were they given court hearings to determine their guilt or innocence, a flagrant denial of American justice. (*The Challenge of Democracy*)

In 1942, shortly after the beginning of World War II, all Japanese living on the West Coast were evacuated inland. Some 120,000 persons, at least two-thirds of whom were *native-born American citizens,* were involved. These people were interned in "war relocation camps" operated by the Government. The relocation program caused severe economic and personal hardship for many. In 1944, however, in *Korematsu v. United States* the Supreme Court held that the evacuation program was legal as a wartime emergency measure. The action has been severely criticized ever since. Japanese-Americans fought heroically in the armed forces in World War II, and not a single case of *Nisei* (American-born Japanese) disloyalty has ever been found. (*Magruder's American Government*)

However, there are other texts that neither condemn the government's action nor discuss the loyalty of the Japanese Americans. These texts contribute to the prejudicial thinking that is often the root cause of violations of civil liberties. The following account certainly lacks *balance* and, because of its implications, even *validity:*

At the beginning of World War II, many Japanese-Americans were living in the Pacific Coast military zone. It was natural that some people should be distrustful of them because their ancestors had come from the enemy's country. Was it not possible, they asked, that these people of Japanese ancestry might give their loyalty to their ancient homeland? These Japanese-Americans posed a special problem because many other people considered them risks to our wartime security. The result was that in 1942 the United States government moved about 110,000 Japanese from their homes and sent them to relocation centers far from the coast. Most of these Japanese were native-born American citizens, known as *Nisei.* (*Civics for Americans*)

No matter how much *realism* most passages on Japanese-Americans show, the fact remains that what was true in 1960 is true today. None of the forty-five texts examined, "give equal treatment in terms of factual information to Americans of Asiatic origin as compared with that accorded other groups in the United States."* Only one text offered historical material on this group which did not follow the general practice of referring to Oriental Americans only to illustrate other historical points—for example, the violation of civil liberties or the need for immigration restrictions—and that reference was not in an American history but in a social problems text.

The Asians who came to the United States across the Pacific settled in greatest numbers on the West Coast. There they found many descendants of Spaniards and Mexicans, as well as adventurous easterners who had traveled across the continent as pioneers. Japanese-American farmers, who specialize in growing fruit and vegetables, have helped to turn California into a wonderful garden. Chinese businessmen and artisans have contributed to the rapid growth of such cities as San Francisco and Los Angeles. Both of these nationality groups came to the United States chiefly in the latter part of the nineteenth century and the early years of the twentieth century. Both have had a long struggle to win full

*ADL Study, p. 55.

acceptance in the new world. Both have recently won for themselves the right to become citizens by naturalization. (*Government in Our Republic*)

C. Spanish-speaking peoples

In 1969, as in 1960 and 1949, the Spanish-speaking peoples of the United States are generally ignored by textbooks. Only eight of the forty-five books examined (five social problems texts and three American histories) offer textual references to this group in the continental United States. An additional four make references in photograph captions. The Puerto Ricans in continental United States are mentioned in seven texts, the Mexican Americans in two, and the Cuban immigrants in two. Only six texts offer more than one paragraph of information about any of these groups, and only one mentions all of them.

American history texts flagrantly avoid references to Spanish-speaking peoples. The only clue they give students as to the presence of Mexican Americans in the United States comes from a photo caption which simply states: "Los Angeles, like many other cities in the West, reflects its Spanish inheritance in the names of its streets, in art, architecture, music, foods, fiestas, and in its citizens of Mexican ancestry" (*History of Our United States*). Nor do they do much more for the Puerto Ricans. Only three of the American histories reviewed refer to them, and two of these accounts are so lacking in both *comprehensiveness* and *balance* that they create or reinforce an unfavorable stereotype:

In New York the stream of migration was swelled by additional numbers of immigrants from Puerto Rico between 1940 and 1960. *(Our American Republic)*

The inadequacy of housing in the cities was felt especially keenly not only by Negroes but also by recent arrivals from Puerto Rico. Puerto Ricans had begun to come to the United States in large numbers after the Second World War. Hoping to find better living conditions than those on their native island, they often found themselves mired in new despair. *(The Adventure of the American People)*

By contrast the only American history to offer a lengthy account of Spanish-speaking peoples does so in a "Focus" section, which introduces the Puerto Rican positively in the context of past immigrant groups which have helped to make America what it is today:

A Nation of Immigrants. America is a nation of immigrants. Since the days of the Founding Fathers, many groups of immigrants have come to our shores. These millions of newcomers—from such places as Germany, Italy, Ireland and China—have worked hard and have become good citizens. They have fought in our country's wars, helped to build America's wealth, and enriched our culture.

After World War II, another group of newcomers, the Puerto Ricans, began to arrive in the United States. Within a few years, several hundred thousand of these newcomers had arrived. But these Puerto Ricans were different from past newcomers, for they already were American citizens. This island of Puerto Rico is an "associated commonwealth" of the

United States, and its people have been American citizens since 1917.

Puerto Rico is a beautiful, sunny island in the Caribbean Sea, but it is small and crowded—about fourteen times as crowded as the continental United States. Many Puerto Ricans move to the United States to escape this overcrowding. They also hope to find better jobs here and a better life.

Life is a hard struggle for many Puerto Rican newcomers, as it was for many immigrants in the past. Many find that they can get only the lowest-paying jobs and that they must live in rundown slum areas. Sometimes they have difficulties because they speak Spanish and know only a little English when they arrive. But in time these fellow citizens of ours are absorbed into American life. A great many of them go on to make valuable contributions to American society. The newcomers in our history have always done this. Without them, America would not be the strong and powerful nation it is. (*Story of the American Nation*)

Social problems texts do only slightly better for this group. Only five provide more than a passing reference to Spanish-speaking peoples. The only two accounts which refer to Cubans in the United States are in these texts, but they do not meet the criterion of *balance* as they tell virtually nothing about the Cuban himself. The primary emphasis is on United States efforts to provide a home for escapees from Communist nations. In addition, no reference whatever is made to those Cubans who had settled in this country years before Fidel Castro became Cuba's leader.

These texts also provide the only textbook account of Mexican Americans found in this study. Unfortunately, neither of the presentations does more than tell of the problems of these people. One account covers Mexican Americans only as migrant workers and discusses the "plight" of these people. While it is a necessary and *comprehensive* discussion of migrant workers, it can hardly be considered a *balanced* and *comprehensive* treatment of the Mexican American. The only other text to cover this group tells the student how the "people of Mexican descent migrated to America primarily because they lacked economic opportunities at home and were attracted by the lure of higher wages." It then goes on to reinforce or create stereotypes in a discussion which is couched in primarily racial terms and which pictures the Mexican American mainly as a law violator:

> Since the border between Mexico and the United States is not adequately patrolled, many Mexicans cross over illegally. Because many wade or swim across the Rio Grande, they often are referred to derogatorily as *wetbacks*. Former Attorney General Brownell reported in 1954 that over 267,000 arrests were made for illegal entries. These violations of the law will cease only when Congress appropriates sufficient funds to add men to our border patrol.
>
> The social status of the Mexican is above that of the Negro, but lower than that of the native-born white. Although they have little social contact with the white population, they do

intermingle in business and politics. Juvenile delinquency ranks high among adolescents. And since school attendance laws are not strictly enforced, many children drop out of school early. Segregation also compels them to live in slums and substandard houses. For this and other reasons, their death rate from disease is much higher than that of the white population. (*The Challenge of Democracy*)

This account, with the one-sided image it invokes, fails to meet the criteria of *balance* and *comprehensiveness.*

The Puerto Ricans fare somewhat better in these texts. All of the three accounts available provide positive images of these people while telling realistically about the problems they face in adjusting to a new way of life. Excerpts from two of these accounts discuss the talents of the Puerto Ricans and remind students that they have much to offer:

At the same time schools in the area offered courses in English and vocational training. In the meantime Puerto Ricans are beginning to show talent in running their own businesses.

Puerto Ricans are here to stay, but in the early 1960's the expansion of industry by American business in Puerto Rico brought a substantial reduction in migration to the states. Today more than 700 new manufacturing plants offer Puerto Ricans thousands of new jobs in their homeland. American businessmen train Puerto Ricans for management as soon as possible. (*Your Life as a Citizen*)

The Puerto Ricans are gradually learning to adapt themselves to their new environment. Some adults go to special schools where they can learn English and acquire trade skills. But there should be a greater effort on the part of each community where Puerto Ricans have settled to make them welcome. We should realize that these people, like those who come to us from foreign lands, have much to give us in the way of cultural contributions. (*Civics for Americans*)

A third account meets the criteria of *realism* and *comprehensiveness* in explaining the problems that face the Puerto Rican—the need for mothers to work, the language barrier, racial discrimination—in the case of dark-skinned Puerto Ricans—and the crowded living conditions they must endure. This account goes on further to *balance* its presentation by telling of such positive factors as "strong family loyalty" and the contributions Puerto Ricans have made to our labor forces "in spite of difficulties." It concludes by stating that:

> Some have distinguished themselves by superior performances: for example, José Ferrer and Juando Hernandez in the movies and on the stage, Jesus Maria Sanromá in music, and Rubén Gomez in baseball. (*Problems of Democracy*)

Thus the 1960 report's criticisms still apply. Only a small number of texts mention Spanish-speaking peoples. Several of these books do so in such a way as to leave the reader with an impression that is both negative and one-sided. With the exception of the four accounts presented in these pages, information on the positive attributes and contributions of these peoples is not available.

SUMMARY

As compared with findings of previous studies, the treatment of the minority groups in the textbooks reviewed had the following characteristics:

A. In general the treatment of the American Indians has changed markedly since 1949. Accounts of white deceit and of Indian culture abound as they never had in the past. However, much more progress is still desirable. References to the Indian in contemporary society are frequently missing, and those that do appear rarely appraise accurately the current state of these people. In addition, some few histories continue to give the impression that the Indians were justifiably overcome by explorers and settlers.

B. There has been virtually no improvement in the textbook treatment of Americans of Oriental descent. The achievements, varied characteristics, and current status of Chinese Americans and Japanese Americans are still a neglected subject. Textbook portrayals continue to be used primarily in the context of other events in American history. On the whole, the image of the Chinese American is the same: that of an outsider presenting a threat to the living standard of native Americans. Japanese Americans are depicted at best as those who suffered a breach of civil liberties in World War II, but nevertheless performed loyally for the American cause. Their origins and past and present achievements are uniformly neglected.

C. Practically no attention is yet paid to America's increasingly significant Spanish-speaking peoples. Nothing favorable is said about the Mexican Americans or the Cuban immigrants, and in all references to the Mexican Americans a negative image is conveyed. The Puerto Rican received the bulk of the attention given the Spanish-speaking peoples. In some cases favorable traits are portrayed, but in several instances negative stereotypes are still presented.

CONCLUSION

This study was undertaken to determine what progress, if any, has been made in textbook treatment of minority groups since the completion of the original ADL report on this topic in late 1960.

The current report is based on findings from forty-five leading junior and senior high school social studies textbooks. All forty-five were analyzed for their presentations of Jews, Nazi persecutions, black Americans, and Americans of Indian, Oriental, and Spanish-speaking heritage. The goal has been to illustrate the range of quality in the textual treatment of these subjects by presenting relevant excerpts from the texts themselves.

Although there have been some genuine improvements in the textbook presentations of the topics examined it has been an uneven improvement at best. A significant number of texts published today continue to present a principally white, Protestant, Anglo-Saxon view of America's past and present, while the nature and problems of minority groups are largely neglected. Only a few books within each subject-matter area (i. e., American history, world history, American government and problems) give a scholarly and fair portrayal of certain minority groups. Although there are a few books of high caliber in 1969, no single book provides an adequate presentation of all the major topics covered by this report.

I. *Material on the Jews continues to suffer from an overemphasis on their ancient past and on the theme of persecution.* Textbook accounts of the crucifixion are still too superficial to dispel misconceptions that may underlie some feelings of anti-Semitism; a few books actually reinforce those misconceptions directly by linking Jews to the death of Jesus. Much space continues to be given to democracy's heritage from the ancient Hebrews and to the progress of the state of Israel, but almost exclusively in world histories. Only a very few American histories or social problems texts follow this practice. Some texts—but too few—have begun to state explicitly why Jews are not a race. Most of them do not present a varied, true-to-life picture of Jews in America today. Only a very few books describe in an adequate manner the past and present participation by Americans of Jewish faith and/or descent in many phases of our national life.

II. *Nazi persecutions of minorities are still inadequately treated.* Nearly one-third of the textbooks in extensive use today omit this topic entirely. Moreover, an additional 50 percent slight or minimize what the Nazis did to their victims. Only four of the forty-five texts fully satisfy all the criteria used by the report. Another nine offer reasonable coverage of some aspects of the topic: Hitler's racist theories, the identity—both Jewish and non-Jewish—of his victims, the successive stages of brutality that culminated in mass murder, the number of victims, and the international reaction and consequences. In general, only the world histories treat the topic adequately. American histories and social problems texts either omit it or gloss over it—along with the opportunity to teach lessons about intergroup prejudice and conflict to their student readers.

III. *The black man's struggle for equality continues to be treated more with complacent generalizations than with hard facts.* While the black man's position in contemporary society is no longer ignored, textbook treatments of inequality and attempts to eradicate it are either missing or, with few exceptions, are weak and noncommittal. The achievements of living black Americans are mentioned more frequently than in the past. Historical references to blacks generally do not reinforce the stereotype of a simple, childlike superstitious people they once created. Yet specific examples of exceptions to such treatment are observable.

Information about the blacks' African heritage is largely neglected. Furthermore, while historical references to blacks in periods other than the slavery and Reconstruction eras have increased, coverage in most texts is still far from adequate. Nor are enough scientific data about race and man's inherent potentialities presented to the student.

The false picture of an all-white America has been changed in most texts through illustrations using integrated subjects. However, not nearly enough of these illustrations are included in the average text to portray accurately our society.

IV. *The contemporary role of other minority groups in our pluralistic society continues, for the most part, to be ignored.* References to the American Indian in contemporary society are very often missing, and almost none of the accounts that do exist give accurate appraisals of the current status of these people. Historical material on the Indians has increased and improved dramatically since 1949. Accounts of the injustice and deceit the Indians endured and the contributions of their culture have largely replaced the earlier concept of the "noble savage" who had to be overcome.

But textbooks do not show the same improvement regarding other minority groups. There has been virtually no improvement in the treatment of the Chinese American or the Japanese American. References to these people continue to be used almost exclusively to illustrate other aspects of American history. Furthermore, many references contribute to unfavorable stereotypes. Even less attention is paid to America's increasingly significant minority groups of Spanish-speaking peoples. In social studies textbooks the Mexican American has replaced the black man as the "invisible American." Puerto Ricans fare only slightly better. Few references are made to these newcomers to the mainland and fewer still are favorable.

These findings are not encouraging in view of the goals called for by the 1960 ADL study. That study urged school personnel to demand and publishers to provide social studies textbooks that :

> 1. Present a pluralistic—rather than a 100 percent white, Protestant, Anglo-Saxon—view of history and of the current social scene.

> 2. Portray minority groups not as "outgroups"—strange, different and isolated—but sympathetically and in depth as valuable, dynamic, contributing elements in our culture.

> 3. Deal frankly with past and current barriers to full equality in citizenship and constructive intergroup relations, and with ongoing attempts to achieve both civil and human rights for all.*

---

*ADL Study, p. 10.

With a few exceptions the texts reviewed by this study do not begin to approach these goals. The only specific area in which recognizable progress has been made is the treatment of the black man in past and contemporary society. We are well aware of the major social movement that has brought about that change; yet for the most part the resulting coverage is still inadequate. This may imply that we should re-examine the fundamental nature and purpose of the textbook.

As a basic survey instrument, the textbook of necessity telescopes, skirts, and summarizes. As a profit-making instrument it tries in its condensations to appeal to the many, not the few. Unfortunately, it appears that the few have been those of us who desire textbooks whose content reflects the ideals expressed in their rhetoric.

The message is apparent; we can no longer appeal to the reason and conscience of those who supply our textbooks. Action must be taken by the concerned consumers of those goods (i.e., the teacher, the parent, and the student). If schools and parents continue to be satisfied with "the best available" texts rather than demanding those that *fully* meet the criteria their use demands, improvements will not be forthcoming. The continued purchase of mediocre texts will guarantee the persistence of mediocrity.

The introduction to this report stresses the role of the classroom teacher in achieving the goal of better intergroup understanding. The findings reported underscore the importance of that role. Accurate presentations that reflect the changing and pluralistic nature of our society are necessary for a proper understanding of our country's history and development. If textbooks, the basic instructional tools, do not meet this function by providing such presentations, then no longer should teachers use other materials to *supplement* those textbooks but to *supplant* them. Only when textbooks that can serve as a basic tool in teaching human relations and understanding are provided, should they be used in the classroom. That is the goal of a viable social studies curriculum—a goal that must be reflected by the instructional materials used.

Therefore it is the recommendation of this report that the Anti-Defamation League of B'nai B'rith and similar organizations expend their efforts to:

> **Continue to produce and make available to schools at low cost, provocative and informative human relations materials as well as historically accurate works that deal with the contributions of all our minority groups to this pluralistic society. These materials should utilize both printed and audiovisual media.**

> **Act cooperatively with other major civil rights organizations to convene and coordinate a national panel of educators and scholars charged to design for each of the subject matter areas covered by this report a model text that is both historically accurate and relevant to our contemporary times and student populations.**

> **Influence school systems to act as agents of change by refusing to purchase a text simply because it is "the best available." Some major large-city school systems have been urged to assume this position, more must be encouraged to follow suit.**

APPENDIX

The 45 Secondary School Textbooks Used In This Study

AMERICAN HISTORY

Allen, Jack, and Betts, John L. *History: U.S.A.* American Book Company, New York, 1967.

Bragdon, Henry W., and McCutchen, Samuel P. *History of a Free People.* Macmillan, New York, 1969.

Canfield, Leon H., and Wilder, Howard B. *The Making of Modern America.* Houghton Mifflin, Boston, 1968.

Casner, Mabel B., and Gabriel, Ralph H. *Story of the American Nation.* Harcourt, Brace and World, New York, 1967.

Current, Richard N.; De Conde, Alexander; and Dante, Harris L. *United States History.* Scott, Foresman, Glenview, Illinois, 1967.

Eibling, Harold H.; King, Fred M.; and Harlow, James. *History of Our United States.* Laidlaw Brothers, River Forest, Illinois, 1969.

Graff, Henry F. *The Free and the Brave.* Rand McNally, Chicago, 1967.

Graff, Henry F., and Krout, John A. *The Adventure of the American People.* Rand McNally, Chicago, 1968.

Kownslar, Allan O., and Frizzle, Donald B. *Discovering American History.* Holt, Rinehart and Winston, New York, 1967.

144

Link, Arthur S., and Muzzey, David S. *Our American Republic,* Ginn, Boston, 1966.

Shafer, Boyd C.; McLemore, Richard A.; Augspurger, Everett; and Finkelstein, Milton. *A High School History of Modern America.* Laidlaw Brothers, River Forest, Illinois, 1969.

Todd, Lewis, and Curti, Paul. *Rise of the American Nation.* Harcourt, Brace and World, New York, 1969.

Wade, Richard C.; Wilder, Howard B.; and Wade, Louise C. *A History of the United States.* Houghton Mifflin, Boston, 1968.

Wilder, Howard B.; Ludlum, Robert P.; and Brown, Harriett M. *This Is America's Story.* Houghton Mifflin, Boston 1968.

Williams, T. Harry, and Wolf, Hazel C. *Our American Nation.* Charles E. Merrill Publishing Company, Columbus, Ohio, 1969

WORLD HISTORY

Alweis, Frank. *New Dimensions of World History.* American Book Company, New York, 1969.

Boak, Arthur E.; Slosson, Preston W.; Anderson, Howard R.; and Bartlett, Hall. *The History of Our World.* Houghton Mifflin, Boston, 1969.

Ewing, Ethel E., *Our Widening World.* Rand McNally, Chicago, 1967.

Habberton, William; Roth, Lawrence V.; and Spears, William R. *World History and Cultures: The Story of Man's Achievements.* Laidlaw Brothers, River Forest, Illinois, 1966.

Leinwand, Gerald. *The Pageant of World History.* Allyn and Bacon, Boston, 1968.

Magenis, Alice, and Appel, John C. *A History of*

the World. American Book Company, New York, 1963.

Mazour, Anatole G. and Peoples, John M. *Men and Nations*. Harcourt, Brace and World, New York, 1968.

Petrovich, Michael B., and Curtin, Philip D. *The Human Achievement*. Silver Burdett, Morristown, New Jersey, 1967.

Platt, Nathaniel, and Drummond, Muriel J. *Our World Through the Ages*. Prentice-Hall, Englewood Cliffs, New Jersey, 1967.

Roehm, A. Wesley; Buske, Morris R.; Webster, Hutton; and Wesley, Edgar B. *The Record of Mankind*. D. C. Heath, Boston, 1970.

Rogers, Lester B.; Adams, Fay; and Brown, Walker. *Story of Nations*. Holt, Rinehart and Winston, New York, 1968.

Roselle, Daniel. *A World History: A Cultural Approach*. Ginn, Boston, 1969.

Stavrianos, Leften S.; Andrews, Loretta K.; Blanksten, George I.; Hachett, Roger F.; Leppert, Ella C.; Murphy, Paul L.; and Smith, Lacey B. *A Global History of Man*. Allyn and Bacon, Boston, 1968.

Wallbank, T. Walter, and Schrier, Arnold. *Living World History*. Scott, Foresman, Glenview, Illinois, 1969.

Welty, Paul Thomas. *Man's Cultural Heritage*. Lippincott, Philadelphia, 1969.

SOCIAL PROBLEMS AND CIVICS

Blaich, Theodore P., and Baumgartner, Joseph C. *The Challenge of Democracy*. McGraw-Hill, New York, 1966.

Bollens, John C. *Communities and Government in a Changing World.* Rand McNally, Chicago, 1966.

Brown, Stuart G., and Peltier, Charles L. *Government in Our Republic.* Macmillan, New York, 1967.

Bruntz, George G., and Edgerton, Ronald B. *Understanding Our Government.* Ginn, Boston, 1968.

Clark, Nadine I.; Gruenwald. W. L.; Edmonson, James B.; and Dondineau, Arthur. *Civics for Americans.* Macmillan, New York, 1965.

Dimond, Stanley E., and Pflieger, Elmer F. *Civics for Citizens.* Lippincott, Philadelphia, 1965.

Dunwiddie, William E. *Problems of Democracy.* Ginn, Boston, 1967.

Haefner, John H.; Bruce, Harold R.; and Carr, Robert K. *Our Living Government.* Scott, Foresman, Glenview, Illinois, 1967.

Hartley, William, and Vincent, William S. *American Civics.* Harcourt, Brace and World, New York, 1970.

Hughes, Ray O., and Pullen, C. H. W. (Revised by McCrocklin, James H.) *Building Citizenship.* Allyn and Bacon, Boston, 1966.

Ludlum, Robert P.; Patterson, Franklin; Jeffrey, Eber W.; and Shick, Allen. *American Government.* Houghton Mifflin, Boston, 1969.

McClenaghan, William A. *Magruder's American Government.* Allyn and Bacon, Boston, 1969.

Rienow, Robert. *The Citizen and His Government.* Houghton Mifflin, Boston, 1967.

Smith, Harriet F. *Your Life as a Citizen.* Ginn, Boston, 1967.

Warren, Harris G.; Leinenweber, Harry D.; and Andersen, Ruth O. M. *Our Democracy at Work.* Prentice-Hall, Englewood Cliffs, New Jersey, 1967.